Intercultural Education, Folklore, and the Pedagogical Thought of Rachel Davis DuBois

Jan Rosenberg

Intercultural Education, Folklore, and the Pedagogical Thought of Rachel Davis DuBois

palgrave
macmillan

Jan Rosenberg
Heritage Education Resources
Bloomington, IN, USA

ISBN 978-3-030-26221-1   ISBN 978-3-030-26222-8 (eBook)
https://doi.org/10.1007/978-3-030-26222-8

© The Editor(s) (if applicable) and The Author(s), under exclusive licence to Springer Nature Switzerland AG 2019
This work is subject to copyright. All rights are solely and exclusively licensed by the Publisher, whether the whole or part of the material is concerned, specifically the rights of translation, reprinting, reuse of illustrations, recitation, broadcasting, reproduction on microfilms or in any other physical way, and transmission or information storage and retrieval, electronic adaptation, computer software, or by similar or dissimilar methodology now known or hereafter developed.
The use of general descriptive names, registered names, trademarks, service marks, etc. in this publication does not imply, even in the absence of a specific statement, that such names are exempt from the relevant protective laws and regulations and therefore free for general use.
The publisher, the authors and the editors are safe to assume that the advice and information in this book are believed to be true and accurate at the date of publication. Neither the publisher nor the authors or the editors give a warranty, express or implied, with respect to the material contained herein or for any errors or omissions that may have been made. The publisher remains neutral with regard to jurisdictional claims in published maps and institutional affiliations.

This Palgrave Macmillan imprint is published by the registered company Springer Nature Switzerland AG.
The registered company address is: Gewerbestrasse 11, 6330 Cham, Switzerland

PREFACE

The history of education is complicated. Starting as the provision of knowledge, education as a field diverged, especially in the late nineteenth and early twentieth centuries, creating a tension between the providers of knowledge (the classroom teacher) and the thinkers about who should receive what kinds of knowledge, how, and why (psychologists, philosophers, and sociologists). The field of education grew as a science, and an "elusive science" (Lagemann 2000) at best because of the tensions between provider and thinker and within the ranks of each. Teachers engaged in "chalk and talk": lecture and recitation. The thinkers sought to measure the capacities of students through testing, primarily IQ testing, to basically fit children into a variety of molds, especially that of the workplace. Doing and thinking education, in the words of Thomas S. Kuhn (1970), experienced a *revolution*.

The journey of the field of folklore is also knotty. The term "folklore" was coined in 1846 by William Thoms to replace the phrase "Popular Antiquities" and to include the person—"the lore of the *people*," in this case the peasant classes (see Dundes 1965). By 1888, the American Folklore Society was founded, and the topics of interest included Native Americans, African Americans, and children. Folklore's scholars at the time were either "armchair" scholars who collected materials brought to them from the outside or those who entered the land of the lore, and the people to collect and catalog their expressions. By 1953, *The Funk and Wagnalls Standard Dictionary of Folklore, Mythology, and Legend* listed 21 definitions of folklore, dividing it by approach—literary and anthropological (pp. 398–403). While more definitions have been spawned, folklore,

v

like education, has its "doers" and its "thinkers." Yet as early as 1909, there were "thinkers" like John A. Lomax, who went (and still go) into communities and documented the lore of the people (Porterfield 1996).

As educators and folklorists (usually separately) tangled with their fields, other fields grew as concern for health and welfare sprouted. G. Stanley Hall at Clark University worked on child psychology. Freud developed his brand of psychoanalysis. Jane Addams, focusing on tenement life in Chicago, created Hull House as a place, a safe haven for immigrants to negotiate the heady waters of assimilation, and the Playground Movement, a part of "child saving movement," gave rise to recreation centers and organized sport to essentially occupy the child and keep him or her "off the streets" (Cavallo 1981).

Throughout, issues of difference were on the national mind. Immigration brought a variety of peoples from across the oceans, and with each group—Italian, Irish, German, Jew—a ladder existed on which each group started out of the lowest rung and made its way up. It was hardgoing, economically and socially, and it was especially hardest with those who were already on the land, the African, who was always on the lowest rung. And without exception, all looked to the school as a monument to achieving steps up the ladder, and education the means for stepping up in the world.

One woman Rachel Davis DuBois (1892–1993) attempted to bring education and folklore together in order to achieve a common good in this sea of difference. A child of the Religious Society of Friends (Quakers), Rachel took it as her Concern, her mission, to encourage harmony, first as a social studies teacher and then as a graduate student and activist among the "thinkers" of education and the scholars of folklore. This book is her story, an *assemblage* of what she wished for: "Happy Blending," known professionally as "Intercultural Education."

The story is arranged as follows. An Introduction will outline Rachel's life and work and couch it in the work of folklife education. The second chapter is a series I call "snap shots," short descriptions of the fields that impacted Rachel on her journey. Chapter 3 is a narration of Rachel's childhood, her exposure to cultural (including religious) diversity, and early schooling, which leads to Chap. 4, which lays out Rachel's experience in college, her marriage and first teaching job, and her experience to volunteer with the American Friends Service Committee, the Quaker arm created at first to advocate for conscientious objectors during World War I. In addition to this initial function, the Committee also explored schools and communities served by Quakers, one of which was located in the heart of Jim Crow country, It was Rachel's experience of Jim Crow in that town that led her to her Concern, the eradication of racism.

Chapter 5 paints the picture of how in 1924 Rachel developed her first intercultural program after she returned to teaching, the Assembly, and its component parts, the installment of an approach to student (and teacher) experience based on *emotion, intellect, and social* engagement through an introduction to community representatives from various immigrant groups who visited the school. The next chapter accounts for Rachel's 1929 decision to attend Teachers College in order to refine and test the efficacy of the Assembly program. Out of academic and philanthropic interest in the Assembly, the Service Bureau for Intercultural Education was formed in 1934, and Rachel developed a new method and program, the Group Conversation method and the Neighborhood-Home Festival, a community-focused program for people of differing culture groups to meet, share their traditions, and explore their likenesses. As these programs were taking place, Rachel created information on immigrant groups for public consumption. The Service Bureau Board, dissatisfied with Rachel's approach, demoted her from Director to Researcher. As her last act with the Bureau, Rachel was tapped by the Office of Education in the US Department of the Interior and CBS radio to research immigrant group contributions to American life for a radio series, "Americans All—Immigrants All." It was her last act before she involuntarily resigned from the Service Bureau.

In Chap. 7, I describe what I call Rachel's "Great Segue of 1941." After her resignation, Rachel attended in 1941 a self-actualization workshop led by philosopher Gerald Heard (1889–1971). Through meditation and consultation with Heard, Rachel began to think not of her pain over leaving the Service Bureau, but of what could she do next that would at once meet her Concern and the practice she had built up since 1934. This workshop was profound for Rachel, creating a kind of link between a painful past and an uncertain future. Chapter 8 provides the evidence of how Rachel acted on Heard's counsel and along with supporters who had resigned from the Bureau with her formed the Workshop for Cultural Democracy, which did open new doors because it was more grassroots, activist oriented, and focused than the Service Bureau. The group was asked by a school to assist them in alleviating immigrant tensions, and through the Group Conversation Method and knowledge about tradition accumulated over the years, the students, parents, staff, community, and the Workshop created a field program, the *Parranda*, which allowed for the visitation to community members of various cultures to explore and learn Deweyan style—by experience.

To conclude, with Chap. 9, parallels are drawn to establish connections between Rachel's work and the work of today. Instead of calling it Intercultural Education, folklife education looks toward developing "capacities for tolerance" (Deafenbaugh 2017) which entails the development of intercultural respect for self and others. It applies the same emotion/intellect/social approach as well as wishes for experience, response, recognition, safety, and experience beyond the self that Rachel explored in graduate school. In conclusion, the points will show that if it were not for folklore, Intercultural Education would not exist. And if it weren't for Intercultural Education, folklife education would not be welcome in education environments as it would lack structure and planning which is essential to the education endeavor.

Bloomington, IN   Jan Rosenberg

References

Cavallo, Dominik. 1981. *Muscles and Morals: Organized Playgrounds and Urban Reform 1880–1920*. Philadelphia: University of Pennsylvania Press.

Deafenbaugh, Linda. 2017. *Developing the Capacity for Tolerance Through Folklife Education*. Unpublished PhD diss., University of Pittsburgh.

Kuhn, Thomas S. 1970. *The Structure of Scientific Revolutions*. 2nd ed., Enlarged. Chicago: The University of Chicago Press.

Lagemann, Ellen Condliffe. 2000. *An Elusive Science: The Troubling History of Educational Research*. Chicago: The University of Chicago Press.

Porterfield, Nolan. 1996. *Last Cavalier: The Life and Times of John A. Lomax 1867–1948*. Champaign, IL: University of Illinois Press.

Thoms, William. 1846/1965. "Folklore." In *The Study of Folklore*, ed. Alan Dundes, 4–6. Englewood Cliffs, NJ: Prentice-Hall.

Zumwalt, Rosemary Levy. 1988. *American Folklore Scholarship: A Dialogue of Dissent*. Bloomington, IN: Indiana University Press.

Acknowledgments

One day I was talking with my friend, Pastor Angela Brewster, and I told her how lucky I felt in doing my work on Rachel's book. She responded, as a pastor might, telling me no, I was not lucky, I was blessed. Later, in a visit with Rochelle Goldstein, I mentioned how this work on Rachel was a labor of love. Her observation was, "All folklorists' works are labors of love."

Indeed, this work is at once a product of luck, blessings, and a labor of love. And true to form, there are many friends and colleagues who have watched me or helped me on this journey. To Diane Sidener, Linda Deafenbaugh, and Joseph P. Goodwin (1952–2015), thanks are due for their responses and insights throughout this project. They, Lynne Hamer and Betty J. Belanus, spent many patient conversations with me as I was writing, untangling, weaving, and interpreting Rachel's story.

Loretta Brockmeier holds a very special pocket of thanks. We had so many conversations about Rachel's work, and comparing our work in folklore and education, I have lost count. Loretta's skill as a computer researcher as well has been invaluable as she has mined the Internet for so much about Rachel.

The staff at the Immigration History Research Center at the University of Minnesota twin campuses were most helpful in sharing their files covering Rachel's professional development. The staff at the Historical Society of Pennsylvania and the Friends Library at Swarthmore College helped me fill in gaps related to Rachel's work. Conversations with my mentor, folklorist, and historian Sylvia Ann Grider led me to the many resources available such as Ancestry.com and Newspapers.com as well as suggestions regarding contacting Bucknell College, and the registrars at Teachers

College/Columbia University and New York University to flesh out Rachel's educational experiences were extraordinarily productive.

Jim Campbell of Campbell Arts designed the diagrams related to Rachel's program development.

The works of Nicholas Montalto and George Crispin were springboards into this project. I spoke at length with both scholars, and their insights further guided the work before you. Interviews with Ed and Carol Davis and Chris and Jack Mahon who were related to Rachel, either through kinship or Friendship, gave me a unique and nuanced look into Rachel as a Singular Soul.

To my colleagues in the Folklore and Education Section of the American Folklore Society, thank you for your support with this project. I can only hope that this book will shed a light on the value of the need to investigate history to learn how to reflect and forge ahead in newly developing work on folklore education today and in the future.

I am grateful to Jon Kay and Diane E. Goldstein for their time as I wrestled with Rachel's story. While it might not seem to be the case, these two scholars have influenced some of the ways I have thought about Rachel and quietly offered thoughts burrowed in these words. Pravina Shukla, Lee Haring, and Jonathan David provided guidance when thinking about *assemblage*, Quaker practice, and Vedanta belief, respectively. Don Davis at the American Friends Service Committee archive provided invaluable information on the time Rachel worked with the Committee in the 1920s.

Wendy Nelson and Emily Raymer are to be applauded for their assistance with transcriptions. Joel Kaemmerlen took on the project's index with great energy. My sister, Devorah Rosenberg, spent time on too many of my reports on Rachel's progress, and my good friend, Repha Buckman, encouraged my progress, reminding me that this was "Number One" in my work's plan.

My special Bloomington friends, Cindy Kallet, Grey Larsen, and Deb Phelps, were completely patient with my work schedule. I'm so glad we could visit and am equally glad for your support. To my friends in Texarkana, and Oklahoma City, Jarvis and Renee' Watson, Kathy Hendrix, Bobby and Rhonda Hendrix, Randal and Brenda Conry, Ginger McGovern, Pat Reaves, Jean Kelsey, Mary Catherine Reynolds, and Louise Goldberg, many thanks for your friendship while I was writing in your fair cities.

Linda Braus at Palgrave deserves an award for her patient guidance, sense of humor, and support. Over time she became a valuable friend to me, and to Rachel.

Then there are my special guides, Sarah Bullock, Marcia Doran, Cathleen Weber, and the Better Day Club crew who have watched over me with care and wonder over this journey. So many thanks.

I know I have left some of you out; please forgive me. To all of you, though, all thanks, no blame.

Contents

1 Introduction — 1

2 Snap Shots: Discovering Rachel and Fields that Relate to Her Thinking — 11

3 Childhood, Early Schooling, and Exposure to Cultural Diversity (1895–1910) — 41

4 College, Marriage, Work, the American Friends Service Committee, and the Birth of a Concern (1910–1924) — 51

5 Development of Programs and a Career in Intercultural Education: The Assembly (1924–1929) — 63

6 Graduate School and the Service Bureau for Intercultural Education (1929–1940) — 77

7 The Great Segue of 1941 and the Refreshment of Rachel's Concern — 95

8 Closing Doors, Opening Anew: The Workshop for Cultural Democracy, the *Parranda*, and Facing Joseph McCarthy (1941–1953)   105

9 Conclusions: The Past Is Prologue: Notes for Understanding Folklore and Education Considering the Pedagogy of Rachel Davis DuBois   119

Epilogue   137

Index   141

List of Diagrams

Diagram 9.1	The relationship of emotion, intellect, and social action to tolerance/sympathy/respect	121
Diagram 9.2	The interaction of invite, inform, incite, and influence and tolerance/sympathy/respect	122
Diagram 9.3	Outgrown of the work of intercultural education in answering the wishes of recognition, response, new experience, safety, and outer experience	123
Diagram 9.4	Diagrams 9.1–9.3 in a cyclical motion	124
Diagram 9.5	Diagrams 9.1 through 9.4 put together to show the entire process behind intercultural education	125

List of Tables

Table 9.1	From promising to exemplary practice in Rachel's work	124
Table 9.2	Learning communities in Rachel's work	125
Table 9.3	Rachel's life themes and events	126
Table 9.4	Goals of folklore and education and approaches to intercultural education	127
Table 9.5	Comparison of folklife standards that are applicable to Rachel's three elements	130

CHAPTER 1

Introduction

It is my task to first describe Rachel's life and work as they led up to her own revolution. It is her *assemblage* of herself, growing up Quaker, and the events that led to her creation of three school and community programs—the Assembly, Group Conversation and the Neighborhood-Home Festival, and the *Parranda*. These events/activities melded her understanding of how the school worked and how folklore as a people's tangible and intangible expression served student, family, and community. These programs were created between 1924 and 1950.

My second task is to account for the use of folklore in education environments. Between 1950 and today, programs have been executed by folklorists to provide people, student, and adult alike, with opportunities to explore the power of folklife in their lives and in the lives of their neighbors.

And last (but certainly not least) my charge is to explore how Rachel's programs meet with folklife education programs today. I suggest that intercultural education would not have existed without folklore. I contend as well that folklife education would not exist if intercultural education had not been on the landscape.

This is a chronicle of one woman's campaign for education, pride, and harmony among culture groups in the United States. The subject of this campaign is Rachel Davis DuBois (1892–1993), who, through her Quaker belief in pacificism, education, and work toward the common good, guided her to the creation of education programs, the Assembly (1924–1929), Group Conversation, the Neighborhood-Home Festival (1937), and the *Parranda* (1945–1950) under the name of "Intercultural Education" through the Service Bureau for Intercultural Education (1934–1940) and the Workshop for Cultural Democracy (1945–1953).

Rachel's work began in 1915 when she taught at Glassboro (New Jersey) High School. It was there that in teaching social studies that she employed a dramaturgic approach to presenting lessons, having students act out the parts and people of history's great events, such as the creation and signing of the Declaration of Independence. This meshed well with her sense of dramatic flair, which she capitalized on when she was a student at Bucknell College. Throughout her work she employed a dramaturgic model using the elements of rehearsal, performance, and review, which I explore throughout this book. She wasn't interested in the quality of performance. Rather, she saw the dramaturgic as a mode for immersion into the curriculum.

In 1920, Rachel felt a need to become more involved in Quaker activities and resigned from Glassboro to work with the newly formed American Friends Service Committee, in Philadelphia, founded in 1917 initially out of a concern for pacifist participation in war-time efforts (Austin 2009). One of her first activities was to attend a conference of Quakers in London to hear reports of works across the country and world. It was at this conference that she realized a diversity in Quaker faith and practice, unlike what she experienced in the sheltered arms of her hometown Quaker life, and she returned from the meeting with an even stronger desire to serve.

It was in 1921 that Rachel realized her Concern, something Quakers felt they could involve themselves with in work and pleasant duty. The American Friends Service Committee, through its satellite organization on Abolition, sent Rachel to South Carolina to inspect the work of a school organized by fellow Quaker Martha Schofield (1839–1916). It was that trip through Deep South Jim Crow that Rachel got her first taste of institutionalized racism, and it was that experience that gave rise to Rachel's Concern, the eradication of racism. A rather tall order, she whittled her work to include public schools, colleges, and community groups from Boston to New Jersey.

Returning to teaching in 1924 at Woodbury High School (New Jersey), an opportunity to work on her Concern settled at her feet. Each week, students were herded into the auditorium for an assembly on a topic that Rachel perceived as boring. The teacher was saddled with the task of maintaining order, and it seemed that the students weren't getting much out of the experience. It was the lackluster experience of the Assembly that Rachel did what she called "Dreaming Ahead." She envisioned an Assembly program that would highlight and involve peoples of different cultures in and around the Woodbury community who could share some of the history and traditions in their lives. The Assembly would have three basic components: (1) the *emotional*, where the students would actually be in the presence of a tradition bearer; (2) the *intellectual*, which would involve student study of the contributions of the culture groups to America; and (3) the opportunity to meet with the tradition bearer in a *social*, more intimate situation. With this combination, the Assembly was a success.

Emotion, intellect, and social construction formed the basic spine of Intercultural Education. The disks of the spine fortified an architecture of social tolerance consisting of (1) gathering historical and cultural *information* on the culture groups under study to be shared with other teachers and students; (2) *involving* others in planning and preparing for the Assembly experience, including parents, teachers, students, and the tradition bearers themselves; (3) *inviting* assembly attendees to experience some of the culture being present, like sharing foods and participating in a dance; and (4) *influencing* some kind of change in attitude among participants, including a change from a negative attitude to a positive attitude (to be visited in Chaps. 5 and 6).

Rachel's work took place in the heyday of the Progressive Education movement, which was child centered, but somehow didn't focus on the specifics of culture groups as they were practiced in the home and community. Except for John Dewey (1899, 1916), who promoted the experiential and democratic nature of Rachel's work, the key players in the Progressive Education Movement, including Lucy Sprague Mitchell (1953), Agnes deLima (1926), and Caroline Pratt (1970), thought differently from Rachel, given the fact that they were working in private settings with younger children. Rachel held little interest in children's physical development. She was far more interested in social and emotional growth. She lived for discovery through cultural, not developmental, interaction. Given her Concern, she tended to focus on certain specifics such as the traditional practices of Jews and African Americans. In fact, it was her view of Judaism as a culture ran counter to Jewish agencies like the American Jewish Committee, which viewed Judaism as a religion, not as a culture. This was only the first of her problems as her work expanded into a national phenomenon.

Rachel left Woodbury in 1929 to further her education at Teachers College, Columbia University. She refined and tested the Assembly Program with great success, and it attracted enough academic and philanthropic support that in 1934 her work formed the base for the Service Bureau for Intercultural Education (SBIE). The Bureau served as an information clearinghouse on immigrant groups and allowed Rachel to train teachers in the Assembly and teach graduate students at New York University, where they formed a new method, Group Conversation, which supported the Neighborhood-Home Festival, an opportunity for adults of differing immigrant groups to informally gather to talk about traditions in their lives and explore commonalities and differences (Crispin 1987).

In 1935, Rachel, through the Service Bureau, worked with the Progressive Education Association (PEA) to heighten its efforts at becoming "ethnic friendly." At the time, the PEA had been focusing on the child, acknowledging his or her connections to home and community in education. The organization made a concerted effort to include ethnicity in its programs, but Rachel's approach, highlighting ethnicity, first did not mesh with the PEA and so it dissolved the relationship in 1938.

While most of these offerings were successful, there were members of the Service Bureau Board who were disenchanted with Rachel's work. They did not like how she gathered information on a group-by-group basis, not understanding that she was always trying to "blend" diversity. In 1938, Rachel was demoted from Service Bureau Director to organizational "researcher."

Rachel's last act with the Bureau was serving as a researcher for a new CBS radio series, "Americans All—Immigrants All," developed through the Office of Education, which was a part of the US Department of the Interior. Aired between 1938 and 1939, the program consisted of 26 programs highlighting the contributions of immigrant groups to American life. At the end of the run, Rachel submitted her involuntary resignation to the Service Bureau.

By 1941, Rachel was hurt, spent, and angry at what had happened to her. For renewal, she attended a workshop conducted by philosopher Gerald Heard (1889–1971), who advised her to lose her ego and transcend her pain for the betterment of her Concern. She did just that, returning to New York City and started, with her intercultural education allies, The Workshop for Cultural Democracy, a grassroots version of the Service Bureau that was more activist/pro-active in stance. The Workshop used every tool Rachel had developed over the years to assist in the establishment of informed, involved, peaceable schools and communities.

This book will present the development of Rachel's career and the pedagogy she created to deal with the issues of cultural injustice. She ascribed to a broad-brush definition of education, forwarded by the great historian of American education, Lawrence Cremin, that education [was] "the systematic and sustained effort to transmit, evoke, and acquire knowledge, attitudes, values, skills, or sensibilities, as well as any outcomes of that effort" (Cremin 1976, viii). Although she probably experienced some of Cremin's formation (she was in her 70s when Cremin published this definition), Rachel utilized her training in educational sociology, the science of exploring individuals in groups in educational settings, to create a pedagogy in intercultural education. By "pedagogy," in Rachel's time I mean, (1) a balanced experience of lecture with research, (2) an acknowledgment of context in the school and home lives of students and instructors, (3) respect for the needs and wishes of community and individual, and (4) planning for 1–3.

I believe that folklorists working in education can draw from Rachel's work to create a pedagogy for folklife education that is entirely fitting with the unique natures of educational environments. Our pedagogy is diverse, due in part to our lack of experience when it comes to working within the school (and other education environments) as a unique social system, our quest for creativity, and our recognition of community diversity. That being said, we are creative and attentive to the needs of community and its tradition bearers. But we need to be more "immersive" and perhaps more respectful in the principles and practice in schools and classrooms in order to meet certain goals, objectives, and needs supplied by school boards and schools.

In reading Rachel's writings, I realized how my own training in a technical theater could be applied in this project. Before I left Massachusetts in 1975 to study folklore at Indiana University, I was active in technical theater in all aspects of the endeavor, from carpentry and lighting design to serving as a stage manager and assistant director, "holding the book" for the director as she assigned movement ("blocking"). Rachel's writings evoke the dramatics in her descriptions of her programs and the execution and critique of them.

These divisions make up a direct response to the feeling of the master of the minimal and intense in drama, Thornton Wilder (1897–1975). Wilder believed that drama at the close of the nineteenth century had become complacent. A part of this was due to the rise of the middle class who required soothing entertainments. He yearned for the intense, the powerful, and the inciting in playwriting (1985, viii–xi). His play, *Our Town*, was structured for the tension of the stage manager, the actors, and the audience brought together in Grover's Corners. All that was needed beyond the characters was an arrangement of boards and chairs. In the chapters to come, including as in the following "snap shots" introducing the particulars of Rachel's experiences, I am your stage manager and assistant director. It is my job to make sure action is ready to take place and Rachel brings setting and scene to life in her narrations of action and creations (Ionazzi 1992). While her works come out of her graduate studies in Educational Sociology, Rachel's work is a part of the *longue durée* articulated by Fernand Braudel (1980). The *longue durée* is a wide expanse of time punctuated with shorter events or moments. It has no official beginning, and there is no specific end. Rachel's *longue durée* begins in the seventeenth century with the founding of the Quaker faith articulated in the Peace Testimony of 1660. The shorter events and moments lie in her stories of childhood and her personal, spiritual, and professional development, 1892–1993.

The chapters to follow reflect and embrace Rachel's *longue durée*.

While Rachel's narrated experience is her *assemblage* on her *longue durée*, this chronicle is also a form of *historical biography*. Barbara Finkelstein, writing on "Revealing Human Agency: The Uses of Biography in the Study of Educational History" (1998), tells us that "[h]istorical biography reveals the relative power of individuals to stabilize or transform the determinacies of cultural tradition, political arrangements … social circumstances and educational processes into new social possibilities (1998, 46)." She lists three benefits of biographical study that fit well with this book: (1) "a lens through which to explore the origin of new ideas; (2) "a window on social possibility, revealing an array of social choices and alternative possibilities individuals and groups perceive and construct as they grow up, acquire identities, learn, labor, construct meaning, form communities, and otherwise lead their lives; and (3) an aperture through which to view relationships and social change" (Ibid.). Throughout this work, these observations and benefits will be clear as you follow the path ways of Rachel's life and work. It is a historical biography, and it is an *educational biography*, an account of one person's ideals, ideas, and practices aimed to develop critical thinking over a period of time, which for Rachel is organized thematically over chronologically.

Rachel's work parallels her life. In her work she articulated two clusters of action that are embraced by her Concern, the eradication of racism and the promotion of social justice in a cultural democracy. They support her development as an individual who wore her heart on her sleeve and as a professional who was not afraid of shaking the *status quo*.

This clutch of action is fleshed out in the chapters to come. I synopsize the key ones here, and they are explicated in Chaps. 5 and 6. These approaches are the backbone of her thinking and feeling, evidenced at home, in the school and classroom, and in communities:

1. The *emotional*, whereby people would be exposed to people of different culture groups and learn of their contributions to American life.
2. The *intellectual*: the study of culture groups' traditions and history and how they contributed to American life.
3. The *social* consisting of opportunities for informal interactions with the culture group representatives.

To make this happen, Rachel created a "plan of attack." This plan involved:

1. Inform: becoming knowledgeable about what a culture group was and how its traditions and history contributed to American life.
2. Invite: include parents, students, teachers, and culture group representatives to plan programs.
3. Involve: a continuation of Invite, having people involved in planning and participating in programs.
4. Influence: After 1–3, program participants would hopefully have a change of heart, a new, positive attitude toward culture groups that they could share with others.

Through the three approaches and a plan of attack, five wishes would be met:

1. *The wish for recognition*: recognizing people and self for their contributions and diversity
2. *The wish for response*: the opportunity to express attitude and reaction to others and self
3. *The wish for experience*: the chance to explore the world of other peoples

4. *The wish for safety*: the desire to be safe in 1–3
5. *The wish for something beyond the self*: exploring the world of difference

The chapters are as follows:

One: Introduction
Two: Snap Shots: Discovering Rachel and Fields that Relate to Her Thinking
Three: Childhood, Early Schooling, and Exposure to Cultural Diversity (1895–1910)
Four: College, Marriage, Work, the American Friends Service Committee, and the Birth of a Concern (1910–1924)
Five: Development of Programs and a Career in Intercultural Education: The Assembly (1924–1929)
Six: Graduate School and the Service Bureau for Intercultural Education (1929–1940)
Seven: The Great Segue of 1941 and the Refreshment of Rachel's Concern
Eight: Closing Doors, Opening Anew: The Workshop for Cultural Democracy, the *Parranda*, and Facing Joseph McCarthy (1941–1953)
Nine: Conclusions: The Past Is Prologue: Notes for Understanding Folklore and Education Considering the Pedagogy of Rachel Davis DuBois

In exploring Rachel's programs in the school and community, I had my own "discoveries" and "ah ha!" moments regarding my work in folklore and education, where my approach serendipitously paralleled Rachel's. I will present my "Tales from the Field" in four program areas: (1) folk arts in the school, (2) a workshop on cultural awareness for nurses, (3) an in-service program on cultural awareness for a mental health center, and (4) a school fieldtrip. Caveat: these are the ways I do folklife education work. I can only speak for myself. However, perhaps my designs can be taken, too, as suggestions for programs and projects.

A Note on Abbreviations In this account of Rachel's work, her writings and her organizational affiliations will figure throughout. I will refer to them in name and in abbreviated form. These are:

ATSM	*All This and Something More*
GTA	*Get Together Americans*
NIA	*Neighbors in Action*
SBIE	*The Service Bureau for Intercultural Education*
PEA	*The Progressive Education Association*
CBS	*The Columbia Broadcasting System*
PYM	*Philadelphia Yearly Meeting*

References

Austin, Allan. 2009. ""Let's Do Away With Walls!" The American Friends Service Committee's Interracial Section and the 1920s United States." *Quaker History* 98 (1): 1–34.

Braudel, Fernand. 1980. "History and the Social Sciences: The *Longue Durée*." In *On History*. Trans. Sarah Matthews, 25–54. Chicago: University of Chicago Press.

Cremin, Lawrence. 1976. *Traditions of American Education*. New York: Basic Books.

Crispin, George A. 1987. *Rachel Davis DuBois: Founder of the Group Conversation as an Adult Facilitator for Reducing Intercultural Strife*. Unpublished EdD diss., Temple University.

Finkelstein, Barbara. 1998. "Revealing Human Agency: The Uses of Biography in the Study of Educational History." In *Writing Educational Biography: Explorations in Qualitative Research*, ed. Craig Kridel, 45–60. New York: Garland.

Ionazzi, Daniel A. 1992. *The Stage Management Handbook*. Cincinnati: BetterWay Books.

Wilder, Thornton. 1985. "Preface." In *Three Plays*. New York: Harper Perennial.

CHAPTER 2

Snap Shots: Discovering Rachel and Fields that Relate to Her Thinking

This chapter is a reference tool, a description of fields that contextualizes Rachel's work. It starts with the "me," how I came to Rachel, and work into the "we" of the fields that relate to her training and has the potential to affect and effect our thinking. These snap shots are for you to flip back and forth as you read about Rachel. They ask, "What time is it?" and give you the answer in short of the history of watchmaking.

Longed So Far: How I Met Rachel DuBois and the Intercultural Education Movement

In 1984, I received PhD in Folklore and Folklife from the University of Pennsylvania. My dissertation explored the history, architecture, and use of nineteenth- and early twentieth-century school buildings and playgrounds in Philadelphia. I called them "Landscapes of Enculturation," places where children were moved from the street corner into the school and playground where they were to be trained to be productive citizens (1984). In addition to the material exploration of the school buildings and playgrounds, I also interviewed seniors who attended schools in the 1930s. I was also (and still am) interested in the rhetoric of school and playground, and once I completed my doctoral studies, I was able to turn to this topic. In looking for examples of expression about schools, Joe Anderson, archivist at the Balch Institute for Ethnic Studies in Philadelphia, suggested I look at the work of Rachel Davis DuBois and her concern with children of immigrants and the creation of community-based education which served both the child and adult.

I made the conscious decision to explore Rachel in depth because she, like I, was interested in curriculum development that focused on ethnicity and culture. I returned to the Balch Institute to work on DuBois, and spent that time, January 1985 through July 1986, studying her pedagogy and its effects on students and their communities.

In my research, especially in reading her autobiography *All This and Something More: Pioneering in Intercultural Education* (1984; referred throughout as ATSM) I became convinced that folklore and education would benefit from Rachel's work. I found her to be a forward-thinking professional who wasn't afraid to wear her heart on her sleeve. I learned how her Quaker faith guided her creations of programs aimed at the eradication of racism. I thought she was complex, and her impact was not only with her past programs; it is on our work as well as we draw out the heritage alive in peoples, reinforced by the traditions in our midst.

In August 1986 I put my research on hold in order to pursue full-time employment. Between 1986 and 2008 I conducted fieldwork to learn about the traditions alive in Arkansas, Florida, Georgia, Oklahoma, and Texas, and presented cultural thought fortified with student contributions and those of visiting "tradition bearers" living in the various vicinities to fourth graders and high school students. At first, working in the classroom was very difficult because I was acting as a teacher instructing and not a presenter offering opportunities for exploration. Once I figured out the differences between teacher and presenter, I focused on presentation, teacher need, tradition bearer plans, and student desire. From 1987 on, a lot fell into place and the students, their teachers, our visitors, and I had *fun* while the classes were able to know the diversity in their lives and others.

As I was doing this, Rachel DuBois was never lost in my mind. But I was prejudiced, feeling that folklore and education as folklorists were practicing it like I did in the 1980s/1990s was better than what Rachel was doing. I reacted to her work initially as condescending and rife with stereotypes (Rosenberg 1991, 47–56). In 2009, when I finally brought her out of "twilight sleep," I realized just how wrong I was. Rachel was an innovator who knew how to work the education system, and she understood the need to develop a variety of programs that would impact students, adults, administrators, and community members as equals. By the time I realized this, I was able to return to her work in earnest and made two trips to the Immigration History Research Center at the University of Minnesota, Minneapolis, to explore the 42 archive boxes that contained Rachel's education work. These trips, initially suggested by Joe Anderson at the Balch, fleshed out a portrait that, along with three of DuBois' books (1943, 1945, 1950), provides you with documentation and guidance in which she describes her work, supplemented with commentary from me based on my understandings of folklore, folklore and education, and the history of American education.

There was something else I experienced in her writing, and that, simply put, was "support" of community and of the student. What would it have looked like if I were one of her students? Would I be able to listen to her and share her concern and passion for the eradication of racism? How would I have shared her keenness on compiling literature on ethnic and culture groups to be shared within the school and outside to the community? I would like to think that she supported my efforts as someone interested in the world of Intercultural Education.

Before I left Rachel behind in 1986, I called her at her home, Dawn's Edge in Woodstown, New Jersey. I wanted to talk with her about her work and the thinking that went behind it. I think, too, I just wanted to hear her voice: what did she sound like? Little did I know she was profoundly deaf. When I introduced myself and told her I was looking at some of her programs, she bellowed into the phone, "Are you going to do my programs?!" My response, "No, I want to learn about your programs," was probably disappointing (if she heard me). But my curiosity hadn't hit some brick wall. When I left for my full-time job, I knew I wasn't going to leave this. Her work, as I was learning about it was progressive and public, unlike something my private high school would have welcomed, as it wrapped itself in the cloak of progressive education. Rachel and my high school in the 1930s shared the interest, but they came from different planets. My high school and Rachel were both members of the Progressive Education Association in the 1930s (St. John 1986), but they operated from a different gospel, so to speak. The high school tried to emulate the work and thought of John Dewey with its experiential approach: the child learned by doing. In doing so, students built some of the school's buildings and others worked to create maps to examine water usage (Rugg 1950). Cultural diversity was a non-issue because the school was 99% white and belonged to the upper-middle and upper classes. On the one hand, the school promoted diversity in terms of student interest in subject areas. On the other hand, the school encouraged a certain heterogeneity in how it defined what a student from the school represented in terms of social outlook. Rachel was also Dewey-minded, encouraging participants in her programs to join her as equals in her quest and concern with cultural diversity, an exploration of how to work with and not against the infrastructural norm.

In my research, I learned Rachel had two biographers, Nicholas Montalto and George Crispin.

Montalto focused on Rachel's educational history (1978) and Crispin, through extensive interviews with Rachel, laid out her program called "Group Conversation" (1987). From them (in reading, in emails, and in conversation), I still have many questions about the power of developing what Linda Deafenbaugh (2017) calls "capacities for tolerance" in education and community. To this end I will examine the history of Rachel's work and will look at how it is woven serendipitously in folklife education today in Chap. 9.

As Montalto points out, Rachel was a person without a middle ground: she was either loved or hated (1978, 77) for her passion and singularity. I hope the work ahead will provide a middle ground, something of use to folklorists working in education today.

Spiritual Realities: The Quakers

To begin, the Quaker movement was born out of the dissatisfactions of George Fox (1624–1691). Reported (Hamm 2003; Ahlstrom 1972) to be a pious young man, Fox found he did not fit into the practices of most Protestants and Catholics in his native England, and so he went on a walking quest through the country, seeking fellow believers.

Fox's fundamental belief was that in each human there is a light, a guiding, and divine light that forward thought, feeling, and action in a group or individual. It is the light of the Christ Jesus that dwells within the self and soul, and it is found through worship in silence. The practices belong equally to men and women who experience the light without violence and swearing to oaths. Communication is not prefaced with formal ascription: Sir, Madame, and so on. Rather, as equals unto the Lord, members of the religion refer to one another by the first name, and the more formal "thee" and "thou."

The Quakers were a persecuted people on several levels. For one thing they had no preachers/pastors, and women were allowed to participate in the silent worship that is one of the hallmarks of Quakerism. Fox encouraged membership in his new-found faith, and it was found in well over 1000 individuals in the United Kingdom (Hamm 2003). In 1672 Fox visited the United States, and in 1681, William Penn received the charter to settle in Pennsylvania, which according to Hamm opened "the way for the migration of thousands of Friends from the British Isles" (214). Even with the geographical shift, Quakers were still persecuted.

According to Quaker historian Thomas D. Hamm (2003), "Generalization about American Quakers today is almost impossible" (2003, 64). Yet there are five elements to which all subscribe: "(1) worship based on the leading spirit; (2) the ministry of all believers; (3) decision-making through the traditional Quaker business process, in which consensus among members is in place; (4) simplicity as a basic philosophy; and (5) a commitment to education as a manifestation of Quaker faith" (Hamm 2003, 64).

These form the infrastructure of Quaker being. Within that structure are the essentials in dealing with the world at large with simplicity, peace, integrity, community, and equality, or SPICE. Philip Gulley, writing on *Living the Quaker Way* (2013), brings SPICE to light. Simplicity refers to the uncluttered in belief and practice at home and the community (15). Peace comes from heart and mind on earth that believes in the truth of the Inner Light and holding it close to the soul (59–96). Integrity is something one is born to or sought after, and "honesty … which kindly and clearly speaks the truth no matter the consequences or cost" (Gulley 2013, 103).

Community speaks to that which is within the heart and mind:

"I can't think of a nobler and more vital work for the church to undertake than the building of healthy communities in which differences are appreciated and not feared, where past truths are honored, and emerging wisdom encouraged" (Gulley 2013, 155). Add the concept of *equality*, that belief in the light touching the individual and the group.

Combined, SPICE creates "heaven on earth" (Gulley, 157). But building its infrastructure was not easy. In the United States, this was manifest in 1826 when Quakers split into two factions: the Orthodox Quakers and the Hicksite Quakers. The Orthodox adhered to the Bible and Christ-centered practices. The Hicksites followed the mission of Elias Hicks (1748–1830) and were more liberal in the interpretation of what one could do through the Inner Light.

George A. Crispin, friend of Rachel, describes the Orthodox/Hicksite split: "The Orthodox-Hicksite split was partly for political and partly through theological reasons. The Orthodox resided mainly in Philadelphia and could easily get [to their Meeting House] at Fourth and Arch [Philadelphia]. The Hicksite resided mainly in the outlying areas, like South [Jersey], and it was a one hour or more trip by horse and wagon to get to Philadelphia Yearly Meeting where business was done. Thus, the Hicksites had a political disadvantage.

> There were also theological splits: The Orthodox were bibliocentric [sic, read "bible-centric"] and Christ-centered. They [the Orthodox] thought the Hicksite view of the Bible and Christ were outside the realm of Christianity. They accused Hicksites of not being Christians. Actually, Hicksites regarded the Bible as a supreme form of revelation and Jesus as a supreme example of the divine in Man. (Personal communication, 6 September 2015)

> The Orthodox-Hicksite split happened in 1826. Philadelphia Yearly Meeting built two meeting houses. The Orthodox one was at 4th and Arch [Philadelphia]; the Hicksite one was at 1515 Cherry Street [Philadelphia]. Over time the strong feelings subsided. In 1952 the two-yearly meetings joined. They are one today." (Crispin, Personal communication 6 September 2015)

What binds Orthodox and Hicksite was the "1660 Declaration" penned by Fox and 11 brethren on 21 November 1660 (21/11/1660) in Weedle (2001, 234–237). In the Declaration, the writers stressed the ideal that a Quaker would not exercise violence in war and in life. The framers stated that members of the faith would not seek revenge or any violent behavior, that it was counter to the belief that a loving and guiding God dwelled so in a light in the body and soul. Scriptural authority was given in Luke, Matthew, and Revelations, and was most concisely expressed in Isaiah 2:4, " they shall beat swords into plowshares, and their spears into pruning hooks; nation shall not lift sword against nation, neither shall they learn war anymore" (KJV).

Scripture required strength from the Quaker community, articulated in the Peace Testimony of 1660:

> We utterly deny all outward wars and strife and fightings with outward weapons, for any end, or under any pretense whatsoever; and this is our testimony to the whole world. The spirit of Christ, by which we are guided, is not changeable, so as once to command us from a thing as evil and again to move unto it; and we do certainly know, and so testify to the world that the spirit of Christ, which leads us into all Truth, will never move us to fight and war against any man with outward weapons, neither for the kingdom of

Christ, nor for the kingdoms of this world. (Declaration of Friends to Charles II, 1660. Accessed 6 March 2019)

Rachel and her South New Jersey family were Hicksite, which in 1720 was associated with the Pilesgrove Preparative Meeting. In 1929, after numerous modifications to the Meeting House, it was renamed the Woodstown Monthly Meeting.

According to *Wikipedia*, the town of Woodstown was established on 26 July 1882, just a decade before Rachel's birth. It is "an independent municipality surrounded by Pilesgrove Township" (*Wikipedia*.)

Rachel lived five miles from the meeting where she was a member for 75 years. It was this forward understanding of the Light that encouraged her work and her activity in the creation of Intercultural Education, celebrating through exploration "heaven on earth" peopled with culturally different individuals whose heterogeneity possessed qualities of similarity that could be foregrounded in such a way that difference blended into homogeneity that didn't threaten the individual or the group.

Quakers were saddled with stereotype because of their pacifism, plain dress, and speech. They did not take oaths; they would not go to war. While there might have been a seemingly peaceful presence, Quakers lived according to a high standard, outlined in the Bible. They were perceived as being humorless, and this couplet (I don't recall when or where I heard it) is telling: "No more laughter, no more fun, Quaker meeting just begun." The Quakers were not immune to suspicion and criticism. Quaker spirituality thrives on faith, structure, and good works, such as farming, which Rachel's family did with tomatoes and asparagus. Another aspect of Quaker life is the "Concern," a cause one can devote his or her life to. As I will explore in Chap. 4, Rachel's Concern, which is a defining feature of this book, was with the eradication of racism, something she experienced firsthand in 1921 when she visited a Quaker school in Aiken, South Carolina, and a school by and for African Americans in Voorhees, SC, that operated according to the pedagogy of Booker T. Washington (1856–1915), who believed that training in teacher preparation and in the manual trades was the means for African Americans to achieve as productive citizens.

Expressions of belief can be so structured they can drive a person away. For some believers, the structure is located solely in the New and Old Testaments. Quakers and others, such as those Jews who study the teachings of the rabbis in the *Talmud*, have other guides. The Quaker follows numerous instructions, such as, "Dearly beloved Friends, these things we do not lay upon you as a rule or form to walk by, but that all measure of the light which is pure and holy may be guided, and so in the light walking and abiding, these may be fulfilled in the Spirit—*not from the letter* for the letter killeth, but the Spirit giveth light." (Meeting of Elders held at Balby, England 1656, reprinted in *Faith and Practice* of the Philadelphia Yearly Meeting of the Religious Society of Friends, 2007 no page. Emphasis added.) (Referred here as *PYM*).

> Early Friends proclaimed that from the very beginning every person has been endowed with the capacity to enter directly, without mediator or mediation, into an empowering communion with God. They rejected ... the assumption that this communion, which is essential to spiritual health, occur primarily in the presence of designated persons in an established religious institution using sacred language and rituals. Friends, both in individual worship and in meetings for worship and for business, continue to experience the living God only as awe and healing but also in guidance for conduct. Like the prophets of Israel, they proclaim the unity of faith and social justice. (PYM 2007, no page)

Quakers are not a sect, "but are [a people living] in the power of God" (Fox, in Jones in PYM 2007, 91). God is a communicating God. "He is the Great I Am, not a Great He Was" (Jones, Ibid. 91).

This is of value in Rachel's life as she learned to take the Light Within. On the one hand, much was expected in learning how to use that light. On the other hand, it must have been difficult to *accept* the Light. Her childhood reflects this conundrum which you will see in Chap. 3 on her childhood.

A Brief Outline of the History of American Education

The history of education in America is thorny as it is a combination of politics, social engineering, and pedagogy on the *longue durée*. Education has been defined on many levels; the broad-brush definition of the field covers many bases: "the deliberate, systematic, and sustained effort to transmit, evoke, or acquire knowledge, attitudes, values, skills or sensibilities, as well as any outcomes of that effort" (Cremin 1977, viii). For my purposes I will apply this definition among other viewpoints to relay my understanding of the field before 1914 when Rachel started teaching, to 1955 with the demise of the Progressive Education Association to which she belonged between 1935 and 1938 (Graham 1967; *ATSM, 62–98*).

Historian Michael B. Katz expands Cremin's definition to reveal a four-part picture of the education enterprise. He, like David Tyack and Elizabeth Hansot (1982), observes the changes in styles of the field and is in agreement with them that education was a combination of business and the acquisition of information by way of a system in which education professionals and their ilk were "managers of virtue," bringing the child into some sort of popular civilization.

Katz's scheme consists of:

Paternal voluntarism where the upper class exerted pressure on the lower levels of society to conform to current social mores and behaviors, using the least expensive activity, such as the Lancaster School in which students worked with older student mentors to engage in lessons posted around the schoolroom.
Democratic Localism consisted of the operation of schools by self-appointed community leaders.
Corporate Voluntarism, the engagement of single institutions as individual corporations operated by self-perpetuating boards of trustees and financed through an endowment of a combination of endowment and tuition.
Incipient Bureaucracy, which gave rise to the professionalization of teaching, the centralization of school administration, and supervision of school activity (Katz 1987, 24–57).

The issue I take with Katz is that while it's a usable framework for thinking about education's administration, I can't really *see* its application to students. I am trusted to make an educated guess about how the framework worked. From what I can tell, Rachel's education experience before 1910 was a combination of democratic localism, corporate voluntarism, and incipient bureaucracy. Her high school in the Pilesgrove community of southern New Jersey was supervised by her grandfather Charles Davis. Prior education was in a one-room school with one teacher, Wilma Coles, not being Rachel's favorite.

Between 1910 and 1914, Rachel attended Bucknell College, a Baptist school located in Lewisburg, Pennsylvania. Hers was a lonely experience, but the academics part of her experience was familiar as it was measured with the testing protocols developed by E. L. Thorndike (1874–1949) who strongly believed in the efficacy of IQ testing. She was particularly drawn to the statistical in the scientific method which she ably applied in her research.

On the other side of the coin, Rachel was exposed to dramatics in college, which, while an extracurricular activity, struck a chord that she sustained throughout her career. She was able to interweave the scientific with the arts, a rare instance with the arts, sciences, and the humanities.

Upon graduation from Bucknell in 1914, Rachel took a teaching position at Glassboro High School in the Glassboro community in her native South Jersey territory. At this time, she taught using the behaviorist approach of the day where she imparted information and students recited it back to her and they were tested according to their recitations. Yet there was a new approach to teaching coming down the road in which students were given greater control over their curriculum and Rachel was able to bring dramatics into the mix of the school day by having students act out the subjects and people of their lessons.

This new approach was called "progressive," led in part by the philosophies of John Dewey (1859–1952). It consisted of in-gathering of information by teacher and student and application of it to real-life situations such as exploring the power of heat by boiling an egg and noting its reaction to the heat from cold to boiling. Or, the class could go on a fieldtrip to the fire station to learn about the work of firefighters and then documenting the experience with art, social studies research, or even music. It was experiential, based at first with John and Alice Dewey's establishment of the "laboratory school" at the University of Chicago between 1894 and 1904. Its function was "to create new standards and ideals and thus lead to a gradual change in [social and educational] conditions" (Lagemann 2000, 48). In the Dewey school, the children were encouraged to work questions through and to seek answers out based on a combination of his or her intellectual and visceral senses. Experience in these areas would accumulate and integrate into a child's "equipment for living." As opposed to the traditional "chalk and talk" of memorization and recitation, the school was not only a "monument" to learning; it was a social center "born out of our entire education movement" (Dewey 1902, 86) that it involved more than lessons. Education was a social affair, and the United States, or any other nation, didn't function on lecture/recitation alone. The Nation was one of cultural diversity and that the contributions of culture groups had to be applied to the learning endeavor. It had to exist side by side with the science of IQ (DuBois 1932).

In 1919, a group of progressive educators and social liberals founded the Progressive Education Association or PEA. While it didn't have a formal platform, it did work under seven points:

Freedom (for the child) to develop naturally
Interest, the motive of all work
The teacher a guide, not a taskmaster
Scientific study of pupil development
Greater attention to all that affects the child's physical development
Cooperation between school and home to meet the needs of child life
The progressive school a leader in education movements. (Cremin 1961, 1964, 243–245)

By 1938, PEA membership was at 10,440 (Cremin, 196, 257). The majority of members were private school teachers and administrators, guided by their own boards of trustees. Rachel was a member, but she was strapped by the business model of public education expertly emphasized, which didn't happen with her private school counterparts.

Perhaps the trick of bringing the behaviorist and progressive mindsets together lay in the understanding of education as both a business and cultural endeavor. For the PEA this was a disconnect. It wasn't so for Rachel. She knew how to work "the system," and she was able to create connections between school, home, and community, something that the PEA didn't seem to do, and I think this lack of humanity led to its demise in 1955.

But Rachel plugged on, staying on task with the demands of school and district, and a keen understanding of community and community relations. She was not a stranger, and her pedagogy reflected an *emic* state in which she could relate to the school and the students because, in effect, she was *one of them* (Pike 1955), using the 4-I's:

1. Information: The provision of information by teacher, student, and community
2. Involve: Drawing in other educators, administration, students, and their families into the development and execution of lessons
3. Invite: Making sure that parents, community members, educators, and students were invited to participate in lessons defined by the teacher
4. Influence: The meeting of goals and objectives in such a way that lessons learned can be applied in other areas, such as Scouts, Future Farmers of America, 4-H, and adult works in the civic arena, such as Rotary and Kiwanis, as well as in the home and community.

This meant Rachel had to be a salesperson of sorts, for she had to reach out to interested parties and share her works with them, be it in the classroom or at club meetings. To begin, all of Rachel's programs served the immediate, the child. But she was not child centered. She had the information; she was going to impart it. Only when the Assembly came to be that Rachel applied the 4-I's, and they became a part of the rest of her work.

Folklore/Folklife

Folklore has at least two core identities. It refers to content, and it refers to the study of that content. The term, coined by William Thoms in 1846 (see Dundes 1965, 4–5), was intended to replace the term "popular antiquities." "It is more a Lore than a Literature, and would be most aptly described by a good Saxon compound, Folklore—the "lore of the people""—in this case, the peasant class. Often times paired with the identification of the "quaint and curious," the content of folklore is unexhaustive: jokes, riddles, stories, songs, expressions of belief, such as superstitions and religious practice. These are all expressions learned through imitation and practice in one's home and community. Bound in tradition, the content of folklore, whatever it is, is the corpus of practice identified with the past and forwarded into the future at home and in the community.

Folklore, as the study of the content, is framed out of numerous academic disciplines, including literature, anthropology, architecture, religion, sociology, linguistics, psychology, and history. There is no strict discipline that calls folklore its own. Rather, the study of folklore is multidisciplinary; it knows few bounds.

All of this was captured much later in the Congressional American Folklife Preservation Act of 1976, where the term "American folklife" means the traditional expressive culture shared within the various groups in the United States: familial, ethnic, occupational, religious, regional; expressive culture includes a wide range of creative and symbolic forms such as custom, belief, technical skill, language, literature, art, architecture, music, play, dance, drama, ritual, pageantry, handicraft; these expressions are mainly learned orally, by imitation, or in performance, and are generally maintained without benefit of formal instruction or institutional direction (PL 94-201).

Rachel's experiences with folklore's content and approach come first out of her childhood and first years of college. I will explore this in Chaps. 3 and 4. She was exposed early in her life to cultural diversity and expression as there were African Americans and Italians working on the family farm who relied on her for communication with others and other workers who worked and sang. This gave her an idea of what folklore *is*. As a graduate student at Teacher's College and New York University, she studied folklore, and she carried her childhood memories and graduate school experience, primarily from anthropology, education, and sociology, deep into her works, as she discovered how folklore can be a critical response to the world, using expressions that have withstood the tests of time, such as story, song, expressions of belief, and craft.

Rachel's childhood was filled with the stuff of folklore. In Chapter One of her autobiography *All This and Something More: Pioneering in Intercultural Education* [ATSM] (1984), she relates her mother's superstitious nurse. Rachel tells of Bill Williams, one of the African American workers on the Davis farm, had Rachel pen verse which was sent to Williams' sweetheart. In turn, Williams shared facial tricks with Rachel, her siblings, and their friends using his mobile face. And then there was Joe Pignatelli, an Italian farm worker who loved to sing snatches of opera arias.

As a child, Rachel learned about ethnic identity from a grandmother who would ask Rachel where was her "Welsh stick-to-it-ness" when granddaughter was not accomplishing tasks to grandmother's satisfaction. At Bucknell, where Rachel attended college, her social awkwardness caused her great pain until she realized that she was a jokester, and a good one at that. Rachel practiced her jokes alone in the summers at home, and she would return to school at the ready to tell a joke to her schoolmates. Out of this she won popularity in school government and dramatic productions. But she would always remain an outsider, something she would rely on her Quaker upbringing to relieve that pain.

As a teacher, and later as a graduate student at Teacher's College and New York University, Rachel explored the functions of folklore through courses with cultural anthropologist Franz Boas (1858–1942). At this time, the scholarly field of folklore (Zumwalt 1988) was divided into two camps: the anthropological and the literary. The anthropological approach explored folklore in light of cultural wholes, represented in the works of Boas, Ruth Benedict (1887–1948), and Margaret Mead (1901–1978), whereas the literary view was on the texts collected for the purpose of examining oral literature in the studies of folktale and song by George Lyman Kittredge (1860–1941). In Chap. 5, Rachel relates the creation of the Assembly Program as a means for introducing high school students to the contributions of ethnic groups to American life, facilitating presentations by representatives of those ethnic groups, using an anthropological approach. She felt that folklore, as presented in the Assembly program, which was later used in Group Conversation, the Neighborhood-Home Festival (1937), and the *Parranda* (1945), highlighted cultural differences on the one hand and served as a great equalizer on the other, because speaking ahead of her time, *everyone had folklore*, and provided with the right communicative environment, sharing would be safe, informative, and hopefully pleasant.

Folklore is a powerful educational tool. In terms of folklore and education, each shares a similar purpose, the transmission of knowledge, but with differing foci on how knowledge is given. Folklore is transmitted through observation and imitation of practitioners in one's family and community, including aesthetic and group belonging. Information in the domain of education is passed on by a professionally certified teacher who is trained to impart information using the textbook, fortified with classroom instruction. Success is tested, quantified, using tests designed by the teacher and organizations whose mission is to develop standardized tests (Lagemann 2000; Lemann 2000). Out of these instruments, education is made accountable to politicians and education administrators who keep an eye on funding and standing on the world's plate.

As I related in the Preface, by 1953 there were over 20 definitions of folklore (Leach 1953), and new definitions come up almost every day with each new angle on tradition and traditional expression are turned up. This is important as the focus of folklorists' interest has broadened to conceptualize the performative and communicative qualities, from gesture to voice, to hands as well as to relationships with self, individual, and/or community (Hymes 1975; Ben-Amos 1972). In the United States the concept of folklore has been adjusted to include "material culture," the making items related to a traditional community, and learning about "the whole range of folk culture, material as well as oral or spiritual (Yoder 1963, 43–56; 1976, 3–18). The term applied here is *folklife*, an adaptation of the Swedish term *folkliv*. It involves the analysis of a folk culture in its entirety" (Yoder 1963, 43–56, 1976, 3–18). From Amish buggies to New York taxis, from practical jokes to legends, cake to quilt, church services to pow-wows, from rural to urban, folklife embraces all traditional expression codified in the American Folklife Preservation Act (P.L. 94-201), and over time, even more. In terms of an overall definition, I define folklore/folklife (often used interchangeably) as the *critical response* of a group to the world using expressions (such as the ones enumerated above) that have withstood the tests of time.

With folklore, quantification with numbers is not required. Rather, learning by doing, and having the heart to stay in a particular community mindset and tradition is most important. Rachel valued both approaches, classroom and traditionality, folklore and folklife, and was able to blend the two fields to make a case for her work and explore their importance in her quest for the eradication of racism and the creation of respect within and between cultures and citizen.

FOLKLORE AND EDUCATION

Folklore and Education refers to programs designed to expose and celebrate traditional cultural expression to students, schools, and communities. I will restrict myself to the United States.

This cluster of programs is made up of a variety of approaches signified, in part, by their names: *folklore in education, folklife education, folk artists in the schools (FAIS), and folk arts in education (FAIE)*. Each program shares the goal of exposition to variety and promoting appreciation and tolerance in light of concepts of childhood, education, and folklore, where the child is viewed as a sentient being, able to explore the world provided that the environment for doing so is safe, and is a participant in an experience, education, where skills, knowledge, and lifeways are passed on by knowledgeable, (preferably certified) professionals, folklorists, and educators, accepting of the idea that the participant has a mass of personal, traditionally obtained tools, folklore, for responding to the world using expressions that have withstood the tests of time, such as song, religious expression, storytelling, and craft.

The field of folklore and education is dense and somewhat tangled. To deal with this, I present the field with three areas, none of which are mutually exclusive and defy chronology: (1) the classroom and folklore; (2) the tradition bearer, the folklorist, and teacher in the act of doing folklore and education; and (3) the promotion of folklore and education.

The Classroom and Folklore: This focus is on the use of the student and his or her experiences as textbook. Representative here is Dorothy Howard (1902–1996) who, with her students in New York state, New Jersey, and Maryland, collected and studied their rhythmic games and autograph books as examples of poetry and essay writing (1941, 1950, 1977). Between 1939 and 1941 Alan Lomax (1915–2002) harnessed radio technology to introduce students and teachers to the world of American folksong and its ability to describe cultures and cultural practices of ethnic, social, and occupational folk groups, utilizing songs he and his father John A. Lomax collected in the South, which Lomax the son preserved and further collected from students and teachers for housing in the Archive of Folk Song at the Library of Congress. The radio program was a part of the American School of the Air (ASA), initiated in 1930 by William S. Paley for the Columbia Broadcasting System (CBS) (Bianchi 2008) and aired twice a week and during the school day for the students, whose teachers were plied with curriculum and the invitation to send examples of folk songs to Lomax at the Library (Szwed 2010). In addition to the ASA, CBS produced, through the education department of the Department of the Interior, "Americans All—Immigrants All, a set of weekend broadcasts dramaturgically presenting ethnic and culture groups' contributions to American life via their traditions and outlook for which Rachel was the lead researcher."

Another example of the use of folklore as part of the world of the classroom wasn't the classroom but the summer camp. Norman Studer (1902–1978) started a summer camp at Camp Woodland located in the Catskills of New York State. Studer relied on his experience with the traditional cultures of the Catskills to share with campers. He believed in folklore as a means of letting forth the creative spirit in writing exercise and that the experience would forward a sense of cultural rootedness in the campers (1962).

The tradition bearer, the folklorist, student, and teacher in the act of doing folklore and education. This relies on a mutual understanding of folklore, culture, and tradition shared by the folklorist who presents these concepts in the classroom, coordinating classroom visits with tradition bearers (who Rachel considered cultural representatives) who are comfortable with sharing their traditionally learned skills, and the teachers who can and are willing to work with the folklorist and tradition bearer to shape goals, objectives, and meet state standards to fit into the lessons of the teacher's choosing. In this, the tradition bearer, also called a "folk artist," is what Kirshenblatt-Gimblett calls an "indigenous teacher" (1983), whose traditionally learned skill is the medium for the message that we are all ordinary people, and there are always going to be people doing extraordinary things such as craft, song, or foodways. These types of programs are funded by such agencies as the Folk Arts and Arts Education programs in the National

Endowment for the Arts, and their names reflect and emphasize the focus: Folk *Artists* in the Schools, *Folk Arts* in Education.

The promotion of folklore and education. This comes in the form of being a resource and service provider for anyone interested in "doing" folklore and education. From the 1970s on, folklore and education programs dotted the United States, especially when the Infrastructure Grants offered through the Folk Arts Program of the National Endowment for the Arts created a place for folklore and education programming. In 1988, the American Folklore Society welcomed a new special interest group, the Folklore and Education Section. Founded by Karen Baldwin, the Section was originally designed as a networking tool for the many involved in working in schools, museums, and other such venues. As of April 2019, the Section boasts over 90 members and offers sponsorship of panels at the annual meeting of the American Folklore Society. In addition to these, the Section hosts two awards, the Dorothy Howard Prize and the Robinson/Roeder/Ward award for educators, folklorists, and all parties interested in and practicing the work of folklore and education.

In 1993 folklorists, tradition bearers, arts administrators, and educators were brought together to explore activities and needs with the hope of creating sustainability in the field. Paddy Bowman, Founding co-director of the Local Learning Network for Folk Arts in Education, describes this gathering and what happened: "During a National Endowment for the Arts fellowship in the Folk and Traditional Arts Program in the summer of 1992, Paddy Bowman talked with every recipient of a Folk Arts In Education (FAIE) grant to assess the breadth of the field and to find commonalities that would link practitioners. The Director of the Folk and Traditional Arts Program, Dan Sheehy, and the Director of the Arts Education Program, Doug Herbert, decided that the FAIE field was extensive enough that practitioners should come together to meet with Arts in Education (AIE) leaders and pooled discretionary funds to call a two-day Roundtable on Folk Arts in Education at NEA in the spring of 1993. City Lore was contracted to organize and document the conference and to write a report afterward. Forty people (see list of participants in Folk Arts in the Classroom: Changing the Relationship between Schools and Communities, by Steve Zeitlin and Paddy Bowman, download at http://locallearningnetwork.oralibrary/the-archive) came together, with AIE practitioners meeting individually with the FAIE advocates. In the final half-day working session, FAIE folks concluded that work was just beginning and that a task force was needed. Thus, was born The National

Task Force on Folk Arts in Education, which was funded initially from discretionary funds from both Folk and Traditional Arts and Arts Education programs at NEA. Subsequently, the Task Force was funded for a number of years from main NEA funds on a contract for services to the field, and the Task Force joined the ranks of the National Arts Service Organizations. Paddy Bowman became the coordinator in 1993, and City Lore was the fiscal agent until incorporation as Local Learning: The National Network for Folk Arts in Education in June 2006." Today Lisa Rathje is Executive Director and Paddy Bowman is co-Executive Director.

On the one hand, folklorists are teachers. However, very few are certified as teachers. We are *presenters* who using the 4-I's, [organizing] and [making] sense of what … students already know, "putting them in a position to integrate experiences from their own lives and pasts into the larger concept of our shared humanity" (Grider 1995, 184). We become informed and we share information; we involve others to work with us—teachers, students, families, community members; we invite participation in our works, be it as members of an audience or a presenter; and in our desire for a "shared humanity," we hope to influence thought, if just to touch it briefly.

From the above descriptions, Folklore's stuff and study are flexible for educational purposes. It can be explored through language arts (Howard 1941, 1950; Wigginton 1985; Simons 1990; Sunstein 2002). Music is also a valued point of entry (Szwed 2010). Folklore and education have an umbrella of support that also guides through the Local Learning Network. In conclusion this chronicle *will relate how folklore and education has had to rock, roll, stumble*, seeking fits into established educational systems. We seek out venues accepting of our work, such as the public school, the museum, and the charter school. Our work works. Throughout the pages of "Rachel's Book," you will see the common valleys and mountains we continue to climb in the quest for understanding, respect, and harmony.

Educational Sociology and Pedagogy

Walter Robinson Smith (1917, 15) defined Educational Sociology as "the application of the scientific spirit, methods, and principles of sociology to the study of education." "By such study the social laws governing education may be obtained and applied in such ways as will improve our educational practice." Educational Sociology was born out of a respect for the scientific method (as described by Rachel in Chap. 4) and the contributions of individuals to the dynamics of an environment, in this case, the school. Its further purpose articulated by Smith (1917) was two-fold: (1) "the problem of the aim of education; and (2) of organizing a curriculum which should be in harmony with the aim" (Smith 1917, 15).

The first Educational Sociology programs were established in teacher training, or "normal schools" devoted to imparting the techniques of pedagogical practice in Wisconsin and Illinois (Kulp 1932, 551). According to Kulp, there were over 200 programs in schools of all kinds across the country (Kulp 1932, 551). It was E. George Payne who outlined the shape of the field in 1908 for New York University. For him, "Educational Sociology: (1) sought to discover the principles and indicate the practices essential to educational procedure; and (2) sought to explain the social forces, social groups, and relationships to which or through which the individual gains and organizes his experiences or behavior in their relation to the schools as a coordinating [sic] agency" (Kulp 1932, 559).

Educational Sociology explores group dynamics in a social system while the field's older sibling, educational psychology, studies the mind in a social environment. Its champions are Freud, and the statistical team of E. L. Thorndike, J. B. Watson, and Lewis Terman, and their belief in the measurement of IQ. For Rachel's purposes, emotion and social being was an integral part of the system, which she referred to as EQ (Emotion Quotient) and SQ (Social Quotient) (1932). This measurement tool she employed in all of her work.

By 1932 Rachel was a full-time student in the Educational Sociology program at Teacher's College/Columbia University where she refined and tested the Assembly (see Chap. 6). Her supervisor, Daniel Kulp ll, had just published his work *Educational Sociology* (1932) which Rachel consulted regularly. In his thinking, Kulp wove in the thought of Willard Waller published in his book *The Sociology of Teaching*, also published in 1932. Waller and Kulp introduced the idea of "four wishes" adapted from the work of sociologist W. I. Thomas (1863–1947) that would round out the field, the wants of the individual who wished to be a part of the group: (1) the wish for recognition; (2) the wish for response; (3) the wish for new experience; and (4) the wish for security and (5) an experience outside the self (1932, 1967, 135–149). Given the focus and force of Educational Sociology in the school, the school could identify the shapes of these wishes and fulfill them with thoughtful and meaningful curriculum with the intent of introducing on culture groups and promote change in attitudes from negative to positive. From folklore's point of view, this contributes to the functionalism stressed by anthropologists Franz Boas, Ruth Benedict, Bronislaw Malinowski, and Margaret Mead.

In some respects, functionalism was, and still is, a misnomer. It is not something immediately described by a culture group. It is *implied*. Following especially in the footsteps of social anthropologist A. R. Radcliffe Brown (1935), functioning is an etic way of handling information, in this case "education." While schooling and pedagogy were organized according to behavior sets that yielded social and academic outcomes, *how* this happened was similar to how the parts and pieces and how they were handled by a group made the machine work. If a piece or a participant with it went out of whack, it would be the job of Educational Sociology to figure out what went out of place and how the culture group would go about repairing it. Yet it is not the *only way of dealing with the issue*.

Additionally, given Educational Sociology's focus on the dynamic of the school, the field had to walk hand in hand with pedagogy, defined as "the science of teaching." It is a field that has always assumed a process, structure, and function that is guided by an understanding of the dynamic of the school plant which means connecting to information content and community and school world view, and has gone through much change, from the dictatorial memorization/recitation model to the more open and encouraging opportunities for student, family, and community involvement.

A search through JSTOR reveals one article, published in *Educational Weekly* (1884, 20 September). In this piece with no author or date, the following is said about pedagogy: "the following classification is to be made to indicate some of many different channels of study which the teacher's professional knowledge seems to require."

1. The end of teaching, or purpose of the school
2. The Nature of the being that is to be taught
3. The branches of knowledge by the study of which growth is promoted
4. He [sic] must know how to teach, possess a knowledge of the methods, etc.

Little has changed regarding the who and what the educator does, but much has changed regarding the how and why. It is the job of the educational sociologist to explore all these aspects and define the life of the school as an organism defined by time, space, content, and world view.

Pedagogy is not confined to the school. As an act of guidance, pedagogy can be seen in action in several settings, in addition to the school, including the library, museum, theater, and any other place where people congregate for formal or informal edification.

Larry Cuban, writing on *How Teachers Taught: Constancy and Change in American Classrooms 1890–1980* (1984), sought to explain how teachers "ticked." He outlines five situations faced by teachers past and present: (1) schooling and social control; (2) sorting [tracking according to learning ability]; (3) classroom and school structures (ecology of classroom arrangement); and (4) the culture of teaching; and (5) teacher beliefs and implementation of change (Cuban 1984, 240). What Cuban shows is that not much has changed at least since 1890–1980 in pedagogy as effecting social and intellectual change for the child, especially considering Katz's Incipient Bureaucracy.

Rachel's work as an educator followed this arrangement. She punctuated Cuban's scale with her own plans to meet her mission of introducing and effecting cultural being and tolerance while staying in the boundaries of the school. She did not seem to think about the possibility that the school was a "prison." She instead found it a niche for moving forward.

A Singular Soul: Rachel's Written and Personal Legacy

Ever since Rachel was a child, she was told she was different. Her mother told her of the superstitious nurse. In her experience with the Turkey Buzzard as a teen, described in Chap. 3, Rachel felt different from the others because of her unexplained feeling of oneness with the universe. In college, described in Chap. 4, Rachel felt set apart from her classmates because she had not been rushed into a sorority. And once she developed her Concern and her profession as an educator, she was singularly passionate in that quest for the eradication of racism; she was equally passionate in her approach to life, grounded in her Quaker belief, and found understanding of herself as a distinct person. There were those who called her "overzealous" (Montalto 1978), and there were others who saw her as eccentric and "different" (Davis 2014). I choose to call her a "singular soul."

Rachel never cowered in her singularity. She was more than happy to share it, whether it be in family gatherings or in worship where silence was allowed to be peppered with the statements of feeling by congregants. Rachel was not silenced, and she presented herself in speech and in writing.

As a graduate student, Rachel began to create a written legacy that can be divided into primary and secondary sources. She regularly published her thoughts in the journal the *Friends Intelligencer* and the *Journal of Educational Sociology*, and she published guides to doing her projects in three books, *Get Together Americans*, (1943), *Build Together Americans* (1945), and *Neighbors in Action* (1950). Her first article, published in 1927, opened the door for advanced thinking, calling on Quakers to be the bearers of the torch for a peaceful world order (1927, 474): "It ... [is] the God-given duty of Friends' Schools to keep the torch burning which will light the way of those to come, who really will usher in a new day of international good-will." Once she made this call, Rachel intensified her thinking, following both social and historical issues, such as poverty and immigration. In 1932 (467), she fleshed out Binet IQ testing, along with the work of E. L. Thorndike (1904) and Lewis Terman (1919; Lagemann 2000) to show there was an IQ to consider, but in addition to the mix there was an Emotion Quotient (EQ) and a Social Quotient (SQ) that could be manipulated and measured in the creation to create a tolerant human being.

In 1931, Rachel published a criticism of those who believed Friends' schools were superior to the public schools. In "Friends Schools and Sacred Cows," she asked: "By what specific indirect methods already known to scientists are we going to build social controls?" Through testing student cultural attitudes in Friends' and public schools, Rachel concluded that these schools were not any different from each other. This led her to believe in "The Need for Sharing Cultural Values" (1939, 84) where people of different cultures should be encouraged to maintain cultural practices that could be shared with members of different culture groups. Sharing was vital to the longevity of tradition, and tradition was the mainstay of cultural survival.

Rachel completed her graduate school obligations with her EdD dissertation "Adventures in Intercultural Education" (New York University, 1940). This work was a detailed account of the Assembly Program, consisting of the three building blocks—emotion, intellect, and situational—and the five wishes that formed the design of all her programs (1940, 66–68). She outlined the experiment of the Assembly featuring quantitative analysis in 15 eastern schools and one school in San Francisco using Neumann's study of student attitudes toward cultural diversity (1926) that she applied as a pre-and post-test.

The capstone of Rachel's life detail is in her autobiography, *All This and Something More: Pioneering in Intercultural Education* (1984), co-authored with Corann Okorodudu; it is arranged chronologically, from childhood to retirement. According to Susan Balee, the "autobiography stems from the need to construct a durable self, an identity that is clear and clearly differentiated from all others" (1998, 40). It is at once a testimony of Rachel's life, and it is also an assemblage of data that explains her projects. *All This and Something More* is a valuable reference tool relating to Rachel's personal and professional highlights, and I will draw upon it extensively in the pages to follow. It is, however, a kind of sugar-coated document that reveals chronology, hope, and passion, selected by Rachel who is her own *bricoleur*.

The reviews of Rachel's books were stunning. *The Churchman's* anonymous review of *Get Together Americans* claimed, "Whoever desires to do something real toward solving race problems will make no mistake in taking this little volume as the textbook" (1 January 1944, vol. 158, p. 16). Marshall Braydon, writing for the *Springfield Republican* (2 June 1945, p. 4), claimed: "[Mrs.] (sic) DuBois's new book *[Build Together Americans]* is a mine of practical information for teachers, administrators, PTA officers, churchmen, public officials and community leaders generally."

W. L. Mezger applauded *Neighbors in Action* in *The Christian Science Monitor* (21 September 1950, 18): "For those who value every small triumph over prejudice and see the minor successes the portent of greater victories, *Neighbors in Action* is a volume of heart-warming hope... The simple but thoughtful program outlined by Rachel DuBois may light a candle in the cavern of bigotry."

Secondary Sources

The above reviews segue to a small collection of secondary sources: two dissertations, a chapter in a book, part of an article, and two audio-recorded interviews with Friends/friends and relatives. These make up a painting of a person and her development as a Believer, an advocate, an educator, and a pacifist: a person whose belief that given the "right" circumstances, positive change in attitudes was possible.

Dissertations

Two dissertations document Rachel's work from two different angles. Nicholas Montalto wrote about *The Forgotten Dream: A History of the Intercultural Education Movement 1924–1941* (University of Minnesota 1978). The "Forgotten Dream" refers to the work Rachel began with the

Assembly Program in 1924 and the development of anti-prejudice education and the experiences, positive and negative that Rachel endured with the organization she created, the Service Bureau for Intercultural Education established in 1934, the reasons for her departure in 1939, and the disappearance of the Bureau as she designed it in 1941.

George A. Crispin approached Rachel through her work on "Group Conversation," as "an educational [endeavor] for reducing Intercultural Strife" (Temple University 1987) utilizing conversational techniques to highlight differences and entice talk about cultural similarity. This use and function of Group Conversation to be discussed in Chap. 6 was recorded in conversations between Crispin and Rachel between 17 November 1984 and 28 August 1986.

Books and Articles

Historian Diana Selig (2008) explores Rachel's contributions to the Cultural Gifts Movement in her work, *Americans All: The Cultural Gifts Movement*. Selig sees Rachel's work as a part of a larger movement directed toward the benefits of Americanization in the home and community using print media and curricular devices such as the Assembly created by Rachel in 1924 and produced in 1925.

In 2012, my article, "From Me to We: Three Early Twentieth Century Educators and the Development of Folklore and Education," designated Rachel as a "champion" who created safe curricular environments for the exploration and understanding of cultural diversity and its place in the everyday life of students, families, communities, and individuals.

Who Was Rachel DuBois?

As a "Singular Soul," Rachel was a complicated woman. As she was strong in her Quaker belief, she also had high standards for herself and others. Her nephew Ed Davis (11 April 2014) reflected, "she's a different person. I couldn't describe her any other way, I guess. She was her own person... "She would come down from New York City to visit on the farm, the same farm where she grew up [Woodstown, NJ]. Sometimes at night we'd go out and look at the stars. She knew some of the constellations. I guess she was trying to teach me some of that. And then she had her little plant gardens in New York City and she'd always take some soil back with her, every time, help out with her plants" (Davis 2014).

"She was physically fit. If she wanted to go somewhere, she would walk." Mrs. Carol Davis continues: "she couldn't abide somebody that did not take care of themselves. You know she'd see somebody walking and they're slouching. "Stand up straight! Take a deep breath!" "She was always encouraging people: "Stand up straight, you'll breathe better""" (Davis, 11 April 2014).

Mr. Davis noted Rachel practiced reflexology and absorbed a few yoga exercises, in particular standing on her head. She would wake at 4 a.m. and nurse a mug of coffee while waking and writing. Ed Davis visited Rachel in New York City where he got to see Group Conversation in action: "She had a fairly large living room and she had like 20, 25 people in there. Everybody sat around in a circle and she'd start asking somebody, what was your interest or what did you do when you were like 10 years old? So that person would say whatever they were going to say and then she'd go to the next person. So, I guess everybody realized they're all the same" (Davis, 11 April 2014).

While Ed and Carol Davis spoke to some of the ways Rachel was her own person, Jack and Chris Mahon, "convinced Quakers," or converts to Quakerism addressed their experience of Rachel and her prominence at her home meeting place and the larger Philadelphia Yearly Meeting of Friends. In a round-about way, both Jack and Chris expressed a certain amazement at Rachel's popularity among Friends. They understood that she was well traveled, something Woodstown Quakers did not normally do. They also noted that when Rachel visited their Meeting, she often would rise during worship and address her Concern or other matters related to faith and practice (17 April 2014).

In Chap. 6 I explore Rachel's work through her directorship of the Service Bureau for Intercultural Education. While the Bureau, founded in 1934, started out innocently as a research and activity clearinghouse, there were constant worries over finances. An amount of $5000 from the American Jewish Committee (AJC) was given to the organization, but its leaders felt that the Jews should not be featured alongside African Americans, Asians, and others as a distinct ethnic group. Judaism was a religion, a spiritual relationship with God and community. Rachel and the UJC were at loggerheads over this detail, and in 1935, the AJC denied more funds.

It was at this time that the Service Bureau went through a great upheaval. Board members decided the organization would be better off with a male at the head, and Rachel was demoted from Director to Researcher. Her enthusiasm as a singular soul was shifted to disappointment, and she submitted an involuntary resignation from the group in 1941. As a singular soul, her visions were shattered.

When Rachel left the Service Bureau for good in 1940, she took a month-long leave for nourishment beyond what Faith and Practice could supply. She attended a workshop led by the philosopher Gerald Heard (1889–1971) in Los Angeles, which consisted of daily meditation, communal meals, study of Heard's thought, and a one-on-one meeting with Heard. Heard confronted her about her ego involvement in her work and encouraged her to move forward by suspending the negative in her ego (Chap. 7). After the eye-opening experience, Rachel returned to the east coast, and with some friends, she created the Workshop for Cultural Democracy. The mission of the Workshop was more activist than research-based alone, and its first client was J.P.S. 165 in New York City, where the school administration was struggling with the influx of Puerto Rican students in 1945. The Workshop agreed to work with the school to alleviate the issue if it would be able to do research in the school. The plan was agreed on, and in using the 4 "I's" presented earlier, a program, the *Parranda*, or "neighborhood party," was born and students visited representatives at their homes to learn about their cultures and traditions (Chap. 8). Through the Workshop, Rachel was able to maintain herself as a singular soul, but this time with greater acceptance from her peers. Her commitment was established, her skills recognized and respected. As a singular soul, Rachel was dynamic.

References

Ahlstrom, Sydney E. 1972. *A Religious History of the American People*. New Haven: Yale University Press.

Anonymous. 1884. "Pedagogy." *Educational Weekly*, September 20.

———. 1944. Review of *Get Together Americans*. *The Churchman*, January 3, vol. 158, p. 16.

Balee', Susan. 1998. "From the Outside Looking In: A History of American Autobiography." *The Hudson Review* 51 (1): 40–64.

Ben-Amos, Dan. 1972. "Toward a Definition of Folklore in Context." In *Toward New Perspectives in Folklore*, ed. Bauman and Paredes, vol. 23, 3–15. Publications of the American Folklore Society.

Benedict, Ruth. 1959. *Patterns of Culture*. New York: New American Library.

Bianchi, William. 2008. *Schools of the Air: A History of Instructional Programs on Radio in the United States*. Jefferson, NC: McFarland Press.

Boas, Franz. 1938. *General Anthropology*. Boston, NY: D.C. Heath.

Boyer, Paul, ed. 2001. *The Oxford Companion to United States History.* New York: Oxford.

Braudel, Fernand. 1980. *On History.* Trans. Sarah Matthews. Chicago: University of Chicago Press.

Braydon, Marshall. 1945. Review of *Build Together Americans. Springfield Republican,* June 2, p. 4.

Celsor, Sharon. 1984. *Folk Artists in the Schools Programs Funded by the Folk Arts Program (of the National Endowment for the Arts).* Washington, DC: Folk Arts Program, NEA.

Cremin, Lawrence A. 1961. *The Transformation of the School: Progressivism in American Education.* New York: Vintage.

———. 1977. *Traditions of American Education.* New York: Basic Books.

Crispin, George A. 1987. *Rachel Davis DuBois: Founder of the Group Conversation as An Adult Educational Facilitator for Reducing Intercultural Strife,* 2 vols. Unpublished diss., Temple University, Philadelphia.

Cuban, Larry. 1984. *How Teachers Taught: Constancy and Change in American Classrooms, 1890–1980.* New York: Longman.

Davis, Ed and Carol. 2014. Interview, 11 April 2014.

Deafenbaugh, L. 2017. *Developing the Capacity for Tolerance Through Folklife Education.* Unpublished PhD diss., University of Pittsburgh.

Dewey, John. 1902. "The School as Social Center." *The Elementary School Teacher* 3 (2): 73–86.

———. 1923. "The School as a Means of Developing a Social Consciousness and Social Ideals in Children." *The Journal of Social Forces* 1 (5): 513–517.

Dorson, Richard M., ed. 1972. *Folklore and Folklife: An Introduction.* Chicago: University of Chicago Press.

DuBois, Rachel Davis. 1927. "The Value of Keeping Peace." *Friends Intelligencer,* June 11, pp. 473–474.

———. 1930. "Measuring and Building Attitudes." *Friends Intelligencer,* June 16 1468.

———. 1931. "Friends Schools and Sacred Cows." *Friends Intelligencer,* June, pp. 506–507.

———. 1932. "Shall We Emotionalize Our Students?" *Friends Intelligencer,* December, pp. 973–974.

———. 1939. "The Need for Sharing Cultural Values." *Friends Intelligencer,* February, pp. 84–85.

DuBois, Rachel Davis, and Cora Ann Okorodudu. 1984. *All This and Something More: Pioneering in Intercultural Education.* Bryn Mawr, PA: Dorrance & Company.

Dundes, Alan. (ed) 1965. *The Study of Folklore.* Englewood Cliffs, NJ: Prentice Hall.

Graham, Patricia A. 1967. *Progressive Education: From Arcady to Academe.* New York: Teachers College Press.

Grider, Sylvia. 1995. "Passed Down from Generation to Generation: Folklore and Teaching." *Journal of American Folklore*: 180–185.
Gulley, Philip. 2013. *Living the Quaker Way: Timeless Wisdom for a Better Life Today*. New York: Convergent Press.
Hamm, Thomas D. 2003. *The Quakers in America*. New York: Columbia University Press.
Howard, Dorothy. 1941. "'Our Own' in the Classroom." *Story Parade*: 5–6.
———. 1950. "Folklore in the Schools." *New York Folklore Quarterly* 6 (2): 99–107.
———. 1977. *Dorothy's World: Childhood in the Sabine Bottom*. Englewood Cliffs, NJ: Prentice Hall.
Hymes, Dell. 1975. "Folklore's Nature and the Sun's Myth." *Journal of American Folklore* 88 (350): 345–369.
Katz, Michael B. 1987. *Reconstructing American Education*. Cambridge: Harvard University Press.
Kirshenblatt-Gimblett, Barbara. 1983. "An Accessible Aesthetic: The Role of Folk Arts and the Folk Artist in the Curriculum." *New York Folklore* 9 (3–4): 9–18.
Kulp, Daniel H., II. 1932. *Educational Sociology*. New York: Longmans.
Lagemann, Ellen Condliffe. 2000. *An Elusive Science: The Troubling History of Education Research*. Chicago: University of Chicago Press.
Lemann, Nicholas. 2000. *The Big Test: The Secret History of the American Meritocracy*. New York: Farrar, Straus, and Giroux.
Malinowski, Bronislaw. 1939. "The Group and the Individual in Functional Analysis." *American Journal of Sociology* 46: 938–964.
Maria, Leach, ed. 1949/1953. *The Funk and Wagnalls Standard Dictionary of Folklore, Mythology and Legend*. New York: Funk and Wagnalls.
Mezger, W.L. 1950. "Review," *Neighbors in Action*. *Christian Science Monitor*, September 21, 1970, p. 18.
Montalto, Nicholas V. 1977. *The Forgotten Dream: A History of the Intercultural Education Movement, 1924–1941*. PhD diss., University of Minnesota, Minneapolis.
Philadelphia Yearly Meeting of the Religious Society of Friends [Quakers]. 2007. *Faith and Practice*.
Pike, Kenneth L. 1955. *Language in Relation to a Unified Theory of the Structure of Human Behavior*. Glendale, CA: Summer Institute of Linguistics.
Radcliffe-Brown, A.R. 1935. "On the Concept of Function in Social Sciences." *American Anthropologist* 37: 394–397.
Rosenberg, Jan. 1991. "Intercultural Education and Folk Arts in Education." *Southern Folklore* 48 (1): 47–56.
———. 2007–2008. "An Eclectic Schoolteacher: Dorothy Howard as Applied Folklorist." *Children's Folklore Review* 30: 61–68.
Rugg, Harold. 1950. *Teacher in School and Society*. New York: World Book Company.

Selig, Diana. 2008. *Americans All: The Cultural Gifts Movement*. Cambridge, MA: Harvard University Press.
Simons, Elizabeth Radin. 1990. *Student Worlds, Student Words: Teaching Writing Through Folklore*. Portsmouth, NH: Boynton/Cook.
Smith, Walter. 1917. *An Introduction to Educational Sociology*. Vol. 2017. Delhi: Facsimile Press.
St. John, George, Jr. 1986. *Individuals and Community: The Cambridge School, the First Hundred Years*. Cambridge, MA: Windflower Press.
Studer, Norman. 1962. "The Place of Folklore in Education." *New York Folklore Quarterly* 18 (1): 3–11.
Sunstein, Bonnie Stone, and Elizabeth Chisari. 2002. *Fieldworking: Reading and Writing Research*. Boston: Bedford/St. Martin's.
Szwed, John. 2010. *Alan Lomax, The Man Who Recorded the World: A Biography*. New York: Viking.
Terman, Lewis. 1919. *The Intelligence of School Children: How Children Differ in Ability, the Use of Mental Tests in School Grading and the Proper Education of Exceptional Children*. Boston: Houghton Mifflin & Company.
Thomas, W.I. (with Robert E. Park and Herbert A. Miller with a new introduction by Donald R. Young). 1921/1971. *Old World Traits Transplanted*. Montclair, NJ: Patterson Smith.
Thorndike, E.L. 1904. *An Introduction to the Theory of Mental and Social Measurement*. New York: The Science Press.
Tyack, David B. 1982. *Managers of Virtue: Public School Leadership in America, 1920–1980*. New York: Basic Books.
Waller, Willard. 1932, 1967. *The Sociology of Teaching*. New York: Wiley and Sons.
Weddle, Meredith Baldwin. 2001. *Walking in the Way of Peace: Quaker Pacifism in the Seventeenth Century*. New York: Oxford.
Wigginton, Eliot. 1985. *Sometimes a Shining Moment: Twenty Years in a High School Classroom – The Foxfire Experience*. Garden City, NY: Doubleday.
Wilder, Thornton. 1985. *Three Plays*. Harper Perennial.
Yoder, Don. 1963. "The Folklife Studies Movement." *Pennsylvania Folklife* 13 (3): 43–56.
———. 1976. "Folklife Studies in American Scholarship". In *American Folklife*, ed. Don Yoder, 3–18. Austin, TX: University of Texas Press.
Zumwalt, Rosemary Levy. 1988. *American Folklore Scholarship: A Dialogue of Dissent*. Bloomington: Indiana University Press.

CHAPTER 3

Childhood, Early Schooling, and Exposure to Cultural Diversity (1895–1910)

The Oxford English Dictionary (2007) defines autobiography as "an account of a person's life written by that person." The *Dictionary* further defines *memoir* as a "historical account of one's memory of certain events or people." Both are telltale references to an individual's life, spun from events that identify the teller as *bricoleur*, a selector of events that identify the teller as a distinct entity with a need to tell his or her own story. Once the *bricoleur* is satisfied with her selection of events, she creates a story, an *assemblage*, "a collection of different things that come together to create a meaningful and beautiful single unit" (Shukla, personal communication 24 November 2018).

Autobiography, as Susan Balee' points out, is not necessarily an act of historical or cultural informing by "strong" individuals. Rather, the autobiographer or memoir writer has a "sense of self that is so very fragile. Autobiography stems from the need to construct a durable self, an identity that is clear and differentiated from all others" (1998, 40). Rachel, as *bricoleur*, weaves her story as autobiography and memoir. This chapter maps out Rachel's childhood, from infancy, her religiosity, up to early schooling. The chapter is guided through Rachel's account of her life, *All This and Something More: Pioneering in Intercultural Education* (1984). Referred throughout this book as *ATSM*, it is the sole guide to her experiences and her interpretation of them. This chapter will reveal stories, family folklore about birth, upbringing in the Quaker faith, touchstones to spirituality,

© The Author(s) 2019
J. Rosenberg, *Intercultural Education, Folklore, and the Pedagogical Thought of Rachel Davis DuBois*,
https://doi.org/10.1007/978-3-030-26222-8_3

education, and interactions with African Americans and Italians who worked on the family farm in southern New Jersey. On the one hand, *ATSM* is an emic account (Pike 1955)—it comes from Rachel. On the other hand, the experiences, related as facts, or concepts of facts, are an etic approach, given from the outside looking in (Balee' 1998, 41). Emic and etic come together in Rachel's quest to tell a story of her "life and times," an effort to present an *assemblage* for us to use as an educational and historical biography.

Rachel Miriam Davis was born on 25 January 1892, the second of five to[1] Charles (1866-1930) and Bertha Priscilla (Haines) Davis (1871-1964) in Harrisonville, Gloucester County, southwestern New Jersey. They lived and ran a farm in the Woodstown community in Salem County, also in southwestern New Jersey, on property owned by the Davis' since the seventeenth century where they grew and sold tomatoes and asparagus. The whole family worked the crops, six days a week, and celebrated the Sabbath in attending the community's meeting house for worship. It was at the meeting Rachel was exposed to the light within—a hallmark of Quaker "faith and practice," and lived according to Gulley's SPICE: simplicity, peace, integrity, and equality.

The family was not particularly overly expressive in their religiosity, but Rachel did see herself as religious. She didn't write about it, but this one piece, written much later (probably in the 1940s), expressed her feeling of the supernal in The Road to Peace:

> I see a road, it is called the Road to Peace. It is only a road in the making altho [sic] it was started two thousand years ago by the Prince of Peace. Ahead it is filled with obstacles of all kinds of monstrous of giant trees, of steep hills and impassable valleys. They are God's question marks which must be met and solved.
>
> God is calling us to get on the Road to Peace, to stop sitting in the beautiful valley of present conditions, made comfortable for us by the blood of human slaves. He is not asking all to be in the same place, nor to keep even with each other, only to go with Him and He is all along the Road, at the beginning, and the end and mid-way."[2]

Religious belief intertwined with the family concept of childhood:

> [Our] life on the farm at the turn of the century was not fragmentized, it was whole. We knew by experience that back of the loaf of bread was the flour (I saw my mother's hands kneading it; she resisted any mechanical help for that operation for years); that back of the flour was the wheat. We

each did our part in the planting and harvesting of the wheat. As we grew older, we did our part in the stacking and the threshing of the wheat when the golden grain poured into the sacks. We knew, too, that back of the grain was the "wind and the shower" and we must have known with unconscious wisdom that it was at this point that we mortals had to rely on the "Father's will." I knew that my earthly father was good at predicting the weather; but I also knew he could not control it. (*ATSM*, 9)

The child was not the "blank slate" or miniature adult described in Aries' *Centuries of Childhood* (1962). The Davis children were raised through illustration and imitation: "Train up a child in the way he should go: and when he is old he will not depart from it" (Proverbs 22:6 KJV).

In her early years Rachel could be identified with four moments: (1) family folklore; (2) experiences with members of other ethnic groups, primarily African Americans and Italians; (3) schooling; and (4) her quest to understand spirituality and religion.

As a child Rachel was exposed to folk belief through family stories and superstitions. One day while bunching asparagus, her mother asked, "Rachel, does thee know why thee is different from my other children?" "No. Am I different?" I asked. She replied with the humor of disbelief, "When thee was born, I had a superstitious nurse. She said, 'I'm going to take this baby up to the attic before I take her downstairs, so she'll be high-minded.' We both laughed at the superstition" (*ATSM*, 1).

An experience for Rachel that she explored was her sense of self as a spiritual being, "at one with the universe" (*ATSM*, 11):

I loved going into the woods alone. I decided to stretch out on the grass and pretend I was not myself, but part of the earth. I felt I had become one with the universe. As I lay there looking at the blue sky, I noticed a South Jersey turkey buzzard gliding on the wind. How would that feel? I wondered dreamily. The next moment the turkey buzzard was on my chest, looking at me. I can still see its two eyes within an inch of mine. What I felt was not fear, but a kind of oneness. For one split second neither of us moved. And then realizing that it had made a mistake, it flew off, leaving me full of joy and wonder. I got up and did what I've come to call my Turkey Buzzard Dance to express that joy. This single experience had given me a glimpse into the universal oneness of all living things and their dependence and relationship to each other. (*ATSM*, 11)

This was truly an emotional as well as spiritual experience for Rachel, who chose not to share it with family and friends. She was afraid of being judged as odd and "queer," a running thread of feeling throughout her early life. It wasn't until much later that Rachel gained perspective, aligning her personal experience to the words of the psychologist Abraham Maslow: "such experiences are common in the lies of self-actualized individuals; and are the basic function of art, poetry, religion, and all of our creative energies. These experiences are not limited to adults; they come to children too" (Maslow 1964).

On the one hand Rachel places herself squarely in Quaker's embrace. On the other hand, she had questions. While there was self-doubt, there were moments of self-assuredness, related in this story:

> The only time I felt somewhat superior to a fellow student was in our senior year when [a student] believed in the existence of the Jersey Devil and I did not. She came to school many winter mornings claiming she had really seen his footsteps in the snow "where he'd gone up to a brick wall and vanished through it." I thought it was funny and told her it was not at all scientific. The newspapers picked up on the stories of the Jersey Devil and were full of tales of the Pine Barrens woman who had given birth to twelve babies and was pregnant with the thirteenth. The woman was so mad that she cursed the child and hoped it would be a devil, and so it was. Right after birth it flew out the window and has been around ever since.

The Jersey Devil was, and still is, a part of southern New Jersey legend. Somewhere in the story, there is a kernel of historical truth housed in the South Jersey region known as the Pine Barrens (Degh 1972; Halpert 2010). Some believe the story; others, like Rachel, did not.

As a child Rachel was not equipped to interpret her experiences. Rather, she spent time wondering about them to herself. In feeling awkward and insecure, she put on a mask of confidence and resolve. But as she related in her story about the turkey buzzard, she dealt with her insecurities as a child might and maybe as a Quaker, in silent wonder.

Although there is a stereotype of Quakers as a stoic group, that really didn't completely apply, at least to Rachel's family. At Christmas the Haines side of the family would gather for merriment with singing and storytelling from Aunt Beulah that was tailored to adult and child. For Rachel, having a good time was not restricted to holidays. Happy occasions reached into the lives of three individuals in her life: African American farmhand Bill Williams, an African American kitchen helper Eva Jackson, and another hand, Italian Joe Pignatelli. Williams, who could not read or write, had Rachel write out love poems to his sweetheart in Virginia: "Roses are red, violets are blue/Sugar is sweet, and so are you/As sure as the grass grows 'round the stump, You are my darling, sugar lump." Ms. Jackson allowed Rachel to help in the kitchen, and she shared poetry [complete with inflections]: "Little brown baby wif spa'klin eyes/Come to your pappy an' sit on his knee/What you been doing, suh-makin' pies?/Look at that bib you's du'ty ez me" (Dunbar 1980; *ATSM*, 4–5).[3]

Joe Pignatelli would sing bits of operatic arias, and Rachel would help him with his English, although she didn't know what an opera was. Williams would entertain the Davis kids with his facial mobility, contorting his face into many expressions, to the delight of Rachel, her siblings, and their friends. There was "sharing and caring," but there was also a sense that everyone knew his and her social place. There were boundaries to be honored by both Rachel and her diverse friends. It was not a relationship of me over them, per se, and it is hard to say just how much race figured into the equation of the relationships. In reflection, Rachel does highlight the diversity. "Perhaps such experiences were the beginning of my life long interest in race relations and intercultural education—my concern that people from different backgrounds be encouraged to share the best of their traditions and customs, thus building a richer culture" (*ATSM*, 5). But as a child, she must have felt *special*, as would any child would feel from special attention from elders, and that specialness informed the basics of her approaches to appreciation in the school and in the community.

The Woodstown community was predominantly Quaker and Methodist.

> As for the Jews, we never heard of them as a religion; we children thought the ancient Hebrew prophets must have been Quaker or Methodist (*ATSM*, 10). If there was any sin in this, it would be sin by omission—people and their farms were insular and protected from the outside world. Yet, Rachel recognized religious diversity, and given her interest in people, she took advantage of that interest and explored: "Once I went to a Methodist evangelical service. I knew the Lord would not put his hands on me to take me forward, and he didn't. I knew it even though when we children got into squabbles, the Methodist kids would tell us that we were lost and that we would go to hell unless we were "saved"". (*ATSM*, 9)

What made Quaker worship different from those of Methodists and Baptists? How does it "work?" The *Faith and Practice* guide from the Philadelphia (PA) Yearly Meeting of the Religious Society of Friends (*PYM* 2007) offers some insight. "Direct communion with God constitutes the essential life of the meeting for worship" (PYM, 19). By coming to meeting with a clear mind, the congregant can then "center down" with the congregation, and each on his or her own engage silence as a way of opening the heart to the Inner Light. Some services are called "programmed" while others are "unprogrammed." Rachel grew up in an unprogrammed meeting where members then and today experience a vocal ministry in which the member can rise during the service and speak of something that has been weighing on them. There is a sense of witnessing and testifying that is allowed, enabling the speaker to say either his or her piece or her or his peace (*PYM* 2007, 18–19). With no pastor men and women are equals, and both can offer their vocal ministry. There is no baptism, through either immersion or sprinkling of water.

Additionally, there is the "altar call," which for the Baptists, Methodists, and other Protestants is an individual's public act of accepting Jesus Christ as personal Lord and Savior. In Quaker tradition, there is no need for an altar call. God, recognized in Christ, is ever-present in the heart, soul, and hand. Going to meeting affirms this. Praying on one's own or in a group is up to the individual. He or she may practice faith in other terms. Prayerfulness is mindfulness. It requires an emptying of thought outside of God and focusing on the Alpha and Omega, called "stilling the mind and body" (*PYM*, 19).

As Rachel's childhood consisted of farm work, family togetherness, and worship, education was also a part of the rhythm of her life. Rachel's early schooling was rudimentary at best, and she doesn't discuss the experience as she did with her religious life. She first attended a one-room school within walking distance from the farm. Twenty-five students in grades 1 through 8 were taught by Wilma Coles. Rachel and her classmates played in the woods, but other than that Rachel does not recall much education in the "Three Rs." While she enjoyed time outdoors, she detested such lessons as diagramming sentences indoors. And she doesn't even mention math.

Rachel matriculated to a Friends' school, Bacon Academy, in 1905. Her grandfather Davis was on the school board and offered his son assistance with tuition. The Academy became a public high school, Pilesgrove High School. Rachel attended through her high school years, grades 9 through 12 where incipient bureaucracy was rearing its head. It was at Pilesgrove that she discovered the splendors of botany, guided by her teacher Helen Jaquette. The education experience was Progressive in the sense that students were encouraged to make their own discoveries of the lifeways around them. This visceral approach was novel and was destined to be of similar character to the Progressive Education advocated by John Dewey and the

Progressive Education Association founded some 14 years later (Graham 1967). She was caught between the community run—the one-room school, and the more corporately visible experience of Pilesgrove High School. Between those entities was the Friends School, a private parochial situation.

In Rachel's time, rural schooling was undergoing examination and lamentation. In the estimation of educationists such as Betts and Hall (1914), rural schools were not in step with education in towns and cities. Following a cult of efficiency, rural school reformers cried out for schools to respond to modernization on the farm and in the home in a desire to keep people from leaving the farms for better situations in cities—through reorganized curriculum to match the need of farming, to teach beyond the three "Rs," and to fit the curriculum to encourage people to stay on the farm and contribute to the ever-going need for food. If there was to be lecture and recitation, at least make it meaningful to the child who helps in the field and in the house, especially the kitchen. In doing so, one might feel a better connection to society and keep up with change. This idea smacked of Taylorism (1911) in the sense that it was felt that teaching and the curriculum could be reconfigured to meet agricultural need.

What did Rachel know of the world outside of Woodstown? Her childhood and teen years were sheltered but surrounded by history's story in its own *longue durée*, as the nation began to shift from rural to urban politics and economy, from farm to factory. Under the leadership of three Presidents (McKinley 1897–1901; Roosevelt 1905–1909; and Taft 1909–1913), all eyes were on a new political and social revolution focused primarily on urban commerce and city life. In 1892, Ellis Island opened its doors. In that year alone, 500,000 immigrants arrived seeking a better life (Hershowitz 2001, 222). Under McKinley, the nation endured the Spanish-American War in which Theodore Roosevelt and his legendary "rough riders" were in the fray (Gould 2001b, c, 482–483). The civic-minded Roosevelt was a conscientious conservationist, establishing a system of National Parks, enacted the Pure Food and Drug Act of 1906, ensured the continuation of construction of the Panama Canal, and in the end was awarded the Nobel Peace Prize.

Taft was considered a "lame duck" president (Gould 2001a, 760). In effect, Taft, who preferred the scholarly pursuit of the court judge to the political machinations of the Oval Office, assured the steady standing of the works of McKinley and Roosevelt.

Even the Pledge of Allegiance changed! In 1867 the Pledge of Allegiance was introduced into the public schools and throughout public gathering places, penned by Civil War veteran George Balch, who saw an educational aspect to the "Pledge." The first version: "We give our hands and heart to God and our country, one language, one flag." Francis Bellamy adjusted the tone of Balch in 1892: "I pledge allegiance to the flag and to the Republic for which it stands, one nation indivisible with liberty and justice for all" (Wikipedia, Accessed 30 April 2019). This was a huge outside world then, and given its hustle and bustle, it might have seemed out of control as Industry boomed. The United States was a hot bed for business and the arts. For Rachel, there were doors opening before her personally and professionally that she opened and walked through, first with some fear and trepidation and then with a sense of mind and mission once she grasped the complexities of her faith and her spiritual sense of being.

Agrarian life for families can be solitary but not entirely isolated. Life on the Davis farm was deep in the soil, hand wrought, and heartfelt. Writing on her brother Allen's death in 1970, Rachel wrote the following testament that could well have been associated with her father Charles Davis: "With his efficient hands he made life more comfortable for all of us. There was his garden full of dahlias which he grew and shared. And many acres of vegetables—South Jersey tomatoes—there is nothing like the taste of them anywhere" (*ATSM*, 3). There was a connection to the soil, tilled over the generations, and there was a commitment to the light within of God shared in the meeting house and social and political commerce among fellow farmers at Grange meetings.[4] When in doubt, seek, not only guidance from the climate and the land, and farmer comrades, but look within to listen close to the scriptural and the Kingdom of Heaven.

Rachel does not write about the ups and downs of farm life. They were in the mountains and valleys she spoke of in "The Road to Peace." She did, however, acknowledge the greatest challenge for the farmer, the replacement of the individual farmers' production by what she called the "thousand—acre superfarmer." "These new farmers do not measure their fields by counting steps, hands clasped behind their backs. Nor do they judge the ripeness of their crops by smell, touch, sight" (*ATSM*, 3). She does, however, remain attuned to a spiritual realm and her wonder over it. She kept her experience with the turkey buzzard to herself: why? Was the peak experience she had counter to Quaker belief? Perhaps she feared being doubted by her family and others on the farm, that one is just not to have such unexplainable events.

Rachel says nothing regarding friendships. Perhaps this is because farms were far apart, and she had siblings aplenty to play with. She doesn't mention games or any playlore. She was a child, and I doubt she led a sterile childhood. But in talking about key incidents in her life, play and games did not figure into her autobiography.

Throughout these pages, one will see how Rachel's thought and self-awareness figured into much of what she did. Yet, one will also see the development of a strong resolve of a woman who, by taking advantage of open doors, personally and professionally, the world of difference bloomed before her. As a child of the soil, she did not retreat into the land. Rather, in her later years, she took the opposite direction. She found her life's work in the urban domain, the place where people of difference, like Bill Williams and Joe Pignatelli, struggled to make the world their home.

What is to come is reflective, reflexive, and responsive—key in the structure of *assemblage*.

Notes

1. Rachel's siblings: Walter Haines Davis, (1890–1979); Thomas Weatherby Davis, (1893–1964); Amy Beulah Davis Sinnickson, (1896–1985); Charles Toy Davis, (1899–1933); and Allen Howard Davis, (1906–1970). Source: Find a Grave (accessed 29 April 2019).
2. Immigration History Research Center, Box #42: Miscellaneous non accessioned files.
3. "Little Brown baby with sparkling eyes/come to your pappy and sit on his knee/What you been doing, a-making pies? Look at that bib you're as dirty as me." Paul Laurence Dunbar.
4. The Grange Movement was begun in 1867 as a means toward improving relations between members in agricultural communities. It is a rural phenomenon, and a social as well as political organization.

References

Balee', Susan. 1998. "From the Outside in: A History of American Autobiography." *The Hudson Review* 51 (1): 40–64.

Betts, George, and Otis E. Hall. 1914. *Better Rural Schools*. Indianapolis: Bobbs-Merrill Company.

Degh, Linda. 1972. "Folk Narrative." In *Folklore and Folklife: An Introduction*, ed. Richard M. Dorson, 53–84. Chicago: University of Chicago Press.

DuBois, Rachel Davis. 1984. *All This and Something More: Pioneering in Intercultural Education*. Bryn Mawr: Dorrance.
Dunbar, Paul Laurence. 1980. *The Complete Poems of Paul Laurence Dunbar*. New York: Dodd, Mead.
Gould, Lewis. 2001a. "William Taft." In *The Oxford Companion to United States History*, ed. Paul Boyer, 760. New York: Oxford.
———. 2001b. "Theodore Roosevelt." In *The Oxford Companion to United States History*, ed. Paul Boyer, 676–677. New York: Oxford.
———. 2001c. "William McKinley." In *The Oxford Companion to United States History*, ed. Paul Boyer, 482–483. New York: Oxford.
Graham, Patricia A. 1967. *Progressive Education: From Arcady to Academe*. New York: Teachers College Press.
Halpert, Herbert. 2010. *Folk Tales, Tall Tales, Trickster Tales and Legends of the Supernatural from the Pine Barrens of New Jersey*. Lewiston, NY: Edwin Mellen Press.
Hershowitz, L. 2001. "Ellis Island." In *The Oxford Companion to United States History*, ed. Paul Boyer, 222. New York: Oxford.
Philadelphia Yearly Meeting of the Religious Society of Friends. 2007. *Faith and Practice*. Philadelphia Yearly Meeting of the Religious Society of Friends.
Pike, Kenneth L. 1955. *Language in Relation to a Unified Theory of the Structure of Human Behavior*. Glendale, CA: Summer Institute of Linguistics.
Taylor, Frederick Winslow. 1911. *Principles of Scientific Management*. S.I. Forgotten Books.

CHAPTER 4

College, Marriage, Work, the American Friends Service Committee, and the Birth of a Concern (1910–1924)

In this chapter, this blip in Rachel's *longue durée*, much happened, personally and professionally, in which family stories faded, and we begin to experience Rachel coming into her own as a young adult, a teacher, a wife, and as a spiritual and spirited advocate. Emotionally and socially, Rachel's experience was a roller-coaster ride, similar to others in her age group. Intellectually, though, a steady mind was in definite formation.

No one knew why or even how, but Rachel's spinster aunt Beulah Haines got it into her head that Rachel should attend college (*ATSM*, 14). When asked what school would be best for Rachel, Aunt Beulah suggested Mount Holyoke in western Massachusetts. As the family explored schools in depth, what they found was that each school required entrance exams, although standardized tests, including the SAT, weren't established until 1926 (Lemann 2000). Of all the schools, at least six were operated by the Quakers, east, Midwest, and the South.[1] These were not mentioned by the family. Why Rachel didn't apply to any of these schools is speculation. Perhaps, her education under Wilma Coles and then at Pilesgrove didn't prepare her for the tests. If she took the tests and failed, such failure might have been humiliating, a disaster for Rachel who already was prone to feelings of social and intellectual awkwardness.

Yet there was one college that didn't require entrance testing, Bucknell, in Lewisburg, Pennsylvania. The school was affiliated with the White Deer Valley Baptist Church that was formed in 1846 and was and still is a member of the American Baptist Convention (www.bucknell.edu). The school was named after William Bucknell (1811–1890), who brought the school out of financial ruin in 1881. In appreciation of Bucknell's generosity, the school, which was originally Lewisburg College, was renamed Bucknell College. It was, and still is, a small university open to students, of all faiths, and in Rachel's day in the class of 1914, the school encouraged academics, arts, missionary work, and a brisk Panhellenic presence.

The decision to attend Bucknell was made by Rachel's family, the application was sent in, and the school accepted Rachel into its class of 1914. Rachel arrived on campus in September of 1910 not knowing what to expect, academically or socially (*ATSM*, 14). There was no one she could share her faith with, and her attempts at being rushed into a sorority were dashed against the Panhellenic bureaucracy, something she had never heard of before, but quickly realized the implications of not being "rushed."

> To my surprise, I was not happy at Bucknell in my first year. I had not heard of sororities and fraternities at home; but I realized early in my freshman year that if one was not 'rushed' by either of the two sororities, one was of no account socially, and *I* was not rushed! I would look in the mirror and with anguish say to myself aloud, 'What's the matter with me?' At the dining room table, where I sat the whole academic year in the seat to which I was assigned in September, meal after meal, no one spoke to me except to say such things as 'Please pass the potatoes.' (*ATSM*, 14, italics in original)

She was determined to find ways to be accepted and embraced by her peers. Once again, folklore came to the rescue. Rachel discovered jokes, which she memorized and applied to her collegiate interactions.

Rachel collected jokes she heard anywhere she could hear them. On the farm during the school's summer break, she would rehearse the pithy stories alone or to the cattle. Back at school, she would introduce witticisms with the formulaic introduction, "that reminds me." Unfortunately, there is no record of what jokes she told. But she writes she did get the attention of her classmates. A sorority girl remarked on the jokes and their performance, calling her a "wit" (*ATSM*, 15), of which Rachel said:

> My apparent wit did not get me into a sorority. It did, however, help to get me into the dramatic club, to be president of the YWCA, and to be a member of the executive committee of the newly organized student government. By then, I [in her second year at school] I did not want to be in a sorority. ... Although I became a recognized leader in college affairs, I never felt really accepted by the college social groups. That feeling one never forgets, as it recurs again and again as a physical ache. (*ATSM*, 15)

It certainly was a painful reckoning, but in hindsight, Rachel made a connection that forwarded her thought about her association with ethnic groups also affected by isolation: "I have no doubt now that this experience has made it possible for me to emphasize through the years with the many minority group friends I have, especially the American blacks" (*ATSM*, 15). It was a hurtful experience that Rachel didn't deal with until 1941 when, as will be described in Chap. 7, she realized that that pain was holding her back in the forwarding of her life's work. Why was this the case? Why the feelings of isolation amid all this positive activity? To speculate, she was of one belief, Quakerism, in a large sea of another faith, Baptists. Additionally, her Baptist colleagues did one thing that was slightly different for Quakers. The former did missionary work(s) emphasizing the acceptance of Christ as Lord and Savior. The latter, considering "faith and practice," did not spread the Gospel like a Baptist missionary. There was (and still is) the evangelical bent, but there was (and again still is) a greater service component in such areas as health and education. One contributed his or her bit to forwarding social justice (Angell and Dandelion 2018; personal communication with American Friends Service Committee (AFSC) archivist Don Davis, 19 February 2019).

According to school records, Rachel did well in her studies.[2] She excelled in the sciences. Botany was her favorite subject, and she carried over her love of the earth from childhood, hiking on the edges of campus, exploring and memorizing species of plants, flowers, and mushrooms.

"There are two other lessons for which I am eternally grateful to Bucknell: one is the scientific knowledge on which to base my love of nature. ... The other lesson which I learned at Bucknell ... was the beauty of order and logical thinking—the scientific method. ... Observation is the first step; but while we are observing, we are analyzing the data asking ourselves questions. If we pay attention to our hunches about the data, we can, by an act of synthesis make a hypothesis. This might be an answer to our question, but we can be sure only if we experiment. The experiment must be evaluated with as much objectivity as possible, and the results applied again by us and others until the truth is evident beyond a doubt" (*ATSM*, 15–17). This love of logic and method served Rachel well in her creation of the Assembly Program (Chap. 5) and her graduate school research and program development (Chaps. 6 and 8).

Rachel had a wonderful way of merging her interests in the sciences and the performing arts: "To satisfy my dramatic urge, I took special lessons in elocution from Miss Edith Schillinger. I got no college credit for this, but during vacations I gave whole evening recitals in South Jersey Grange Halls and earned enough money this way to buy my clothes. One of the publicity folders for one of those recitals embarrassed me: 'Come and hear Rachel Davis, the Trained Elocutionist!'" (*ATSM*, 15).

Throughout her attendance at Bucknell, Rachel was persistently courted by Nathan DuBois, a shipping clerk also from southern New Jersey. Nathan was anxious to get married; Rachel was not. She was keen on her studies and be graduated with a degree. Upon graduation she ultimately accepted Nathan's proposal, as she began her first job, teaching at Glassboro High School. While Nathan was an ardent suitor, "He told me that he doubted we would have children" (*ATSM* 22). "I remember crying that night after he left, for in my dreams of having a family, I visualized six or eight children with family dramatics and other interesting activities. ... We talked frankly about it and agreed that if we did not have children, I could make a career of teaching, for by that time I enjoyed that role. There was no "women's lib" in 1915, but we did work out a 50–50 marriage" (*ATSM*, 23). In later years Rachel made up for this lack in her life through her teaching and ultimately in her program development (Chaps. 5, 6, and 8), which led to her final relocation to New York City and her divorce from Nathan in 1942.[3]

On 19 June 1915, Rachel and Nathan married in a splendidly arrayed outdoor ceremony arranged by Rachel's mother (*ATSM*, 22–23). Although Nathan was Methodist, he intoned the traditional Quaker wedding vow: "In the presence of the Lord and this Assembly, I, Nathan Steward DuBois, take thee, Rachel Miriam Davis, to be my wedded wife, promising with divine assistance to be unto thee a loving and faithful husband until death shall separate us" (*ATSM*, 23). Rachel repeated the vow, and the marriage certificate was signed. After a brief honeymoon in Swarthmore, PA, they settled in Pitman, New Jersey, close to Rachel's first place of employment, Glassboro High School.

Early in the marriage, Nathan seemed to be pessimistic about himself, which Rachel didn't recognize during their courtship. When they married, Nathan soon lost his job at the shipyard, and he started experiencing colds. Rachel sought out an Osteopathic physician in Philadelphia. The physician's treatments helped (*ATSM*, 24), and a new life plan emerged for Nathan: he wanted to become a bank examiner. "When I asked him about the requirements, he said he would have to pass an examination which would only be given in Washington, D.C. I went with him to Washington and spent three days in a hotel, going over examinations with him.[4] He passed and began his life's profession with a changed attitude" (*ATSM*, 24). Nathan's first assignment as a bank examiner was in Ohio where he was to stay three months. Rachel took note: when she was away, friends felt sorry for Nathan. When he was away, no sympathy was wasted on her. So much for a 50/50 marriage (*ATSM*, 24).

At Glassboro, Rachel taught social studies, using a dramaturgic approach in which students could role-play the scenes of history they were studying such as The Declaration of Independence. She had no pedagogical training since Bucknell didn't have a program for teachers. Rachel taught according to what I call an "empathetic spirit," consisting of practicing what she liked about being taught and avoiding, whenever possible, the aspects of the education endeavor she found unappealing. Employing the dramatic approach to social studies satisfied Rachel's love of drama and her interest in social studies. At least one student, long graduated from school in 1915, remembered Rachel for this approach (*ATSM*, 22).

Rachel taught in the midst of World War I. The nation pulled together in several ways, including the sale of war bonds. This activity ran counter to the Quaker stance on pacifism, and Rachel was brave enough to let her school superintendent Mr. Woods know where she stood on the matter. At first, he gave her permission not to sell the bonds, and she instead engaged in a peaceful contribution to the war effort canning foodstuffs with her mother (*ATSM*, 25). Nevertheless, she recalled a statement from William James on "The Moral Equivalent of War,": "What we now need to discover in the social realm is the moral equivalent of war: something heroic that will speak to me as universally as war does, and yet will be as compatible with our spiritual selves as war has proved itself to be incompatible" (1902, 357–359).

This was Rachel's "first war," and it challenged her core of pacifist belief which she referred to as "spiritual hunger." It brought to light two questions Quakers regularly asked in self-examination: "(1) when differences arise, do you endeavor speedily to end them; and (2) do you have the life and power which takes away all occasion for war?" (*ATSM*, 27). These questions brought to light "four testimonies," such as peace, equality, simplicity, and integrity that I described from Gulley (2013). These queries nagged her.[5] She felt that "The real strength of our country lies not in its military but in the moral and spiritual strength of those—and there are many—who stand for their convictions based on conscience" (*ATSM*, 26). But Rachel was conflicted. She questioned her pacifism, and she broke down and purchased a war bond "to bring the boys home" (*ATSM*, 27).

She was riddled with guilt which took time and prayer to get over, another reckoning she experienced in later years.

Perhaps to assuage her guilt, she paid attention to the plans from the Philadelphia Friends who, in 1917, established the American Friends Service Committee (AFSC) to assist conscientious objectors, and trained a group of Friends to build roads and landscaped properties in France and parts of Western Europe, although efforts did not relieve famine, typhus, and address social problems (*ATSM*, 28). Rachel followed their work and when "The War to end all Wars" came to a close on 11 November 1918. Rachel soon resigned from her teaching post at Glassboro and devoted 1920 to 1923 to the organization that would ultimately give rise to her quest to eradicate racism.

With the war over and a recognition of her own spiritual hunger, the scales began to fall off of Rachel's eyes. In August 1920, the AFSC sent Rachel and Nathan to London to attend the "First International Conference of Friends." Each day the gathering of some 1600 Friends had worship in silence and then there were reports on various Friends' activities from around the world. Rachel was surprised, and perhaps overwhelmed by the diversity of reports. Not all Quakers thought or acted like those in Woodstown. After the conference, participants took a fieldtrip to see first-hand the ravages of war on citizens (*ATSM*, 33). Upon her and Nathan's return to the States, Rachel immersed herself even further into the work of the AFSC.

The AFSC had a number of special interest sections, including the Pennsylvania Committee on the Abolition of Slavery. In 1921, the Committee dispatched Rachel to Aiken, South Carolina, to conduct a site visit to the Schofield School, created by Quaker Martha Schofield (1839–1916) for Freedmen during Reconstruction, and was funded in part with personal contributions to Schofield from northern Quakers. Situated in the Deep South, Aiken, like many Southern towns and cities, resorted to Jim Crow law to ensure the second-class citizenship of African Americans through a complex series of "laws" that kept Whites and Blacks further apart. As a White woman, Rachel might not have needed instruction on the mores of the Jim Crow South. The AFSC did not prepare her for Aiken nor did it prepare other Friends for different kinds of cultural encounters (Personal communications with Don Davis, AFSC archivist 19 February 2919 and Allan Austin, 20 February 2019). She experienced culture shock when she arrived in Aiken, seeing signs indicating separation between "Whites" and "Colored," and with a questioning mind, and given her dark complexion, she toyed with the idea of using the restrooms reserved for "Coloreds." Somehow, she knew better and voided the experiment (*ATSM*, 34).

At the Schofield School, Rachel was invited to speak on any subject she cared to address. She spoke about the London conference and the refugees she encountered on that trip. She wrote "when I finished 500 throats spontaneously opened with the song 'Down by the Riverside ... ain't gonna study war no more'" (*ATSM*, 35).

While in Aiken, Rachel visited another school, the Voorhees Normal and Industrial School, 30 miles away. "Known today as Voorhees College, the school began in 1897 as the Denmark Industrial School for African Americans in the small town of Denmark, South Carolina. The school was founded by Elizabeth Evelyn Wright with the assistance of Jessie C. Dorsey of Detroit and Mrs. A. S. Steele of Boston. Wright, a native of Georgia, had attended Tuskegee Institute in Alabama and modeled her new school after Tuskegee's curriculum. A donation by New Jersey philanthropist Ralph Voorhees in 1902 was used to buy land and construct buildings for the school, and two years later, the South Carolina General Assembly incorporated the school and renamed it the Voorhees Industrial Institute for Colored Youths."[6] This school was run by the National Presbyterian Church with support from the Rosenwald Foundation of Chicago.[7] This school was guided by the pedagogy of vocation propounded by Booker T. Washington, with a student population of 1000 African Americans and faculty. Rachel thought it would be a good way to present the schools in comparison to one another for the AFSC (*ATSM*, 35).

When it was time to return to Philadelphia, Rachel's whole being was affected by Southern mores. Jim Crow was a shock, segregation of the races didn't make sense, especially to a person like Rachel who believed in diversity and its myriad expressions. The experience rattled her enough that she found her Concern, that issue a Quaker could devote his or her life to. For Rachel, her new-found Concern was *the eradication of racism*. At first, she wanted to cast the net of her Concern far and wide. Instead, she settled on the east coast, and the public school where children's dispositions might be more amenable to change, a nod to the Child Saving Movement advocated by Jane Addams, and other liberal citizens and organizations (Cavallo 1981).

Upon her return to Philadelphia, Rachel presented her experiences to fellow Friends. She also read voraciously about African American culture. She realized that while there was this racial antipathy, she didn't know much in terms of context. She also decided that books and articles alone would not be entirely informative. To this end, she recommended to the AFSC a Committee on Race Relations. The Committee was created to overcome negative attitudes not only from communities at large but within the ranks of Friends as well. There were questions: if Friends Schools are so liberal, why were there so few if any students from African American and other backgrounds? (*ATSM*, 38) How would a Committee on Race Relations become involved with non-Friends organizations? These were difficult questions as they challenged some of the basic tenets of Quaker faith and practice. And with difficult questions, there were no easy answers.

But Rachel was resilient and resourceful. She organized a trip for the Committee to Greensboro, North Carolina, to attend a lecture by Dr. Mordekai, [sic] President of Howard University (now a historic Black college), who challenged the Committee and other Friends attendees to be more inclusive in organizations, the Friends Schools being the most obvious (*ATSM*, 38).

When Rachel came home from Aiken, she met Crystal Bird, an African American woman from the YWCA and the AFSC, and they bonded. As a fellow Quaker activist, Bird was also a singer who brought home the importance of music as an agent of change. The Committee hoped to "borrow" Bird from the YWCA to share her testimony of tolerance to Friends' assemblies (*ATSM*, 39), bringing to light the experience of an African American woman to those who may not have heard someone of her ethnicity as well as how her testimony could be relayed through the power of song. Rachel already knew this power—she experienced it when she visited the Schofield School. That knowledge, along with the friendship between her and Bird, would carry over into the work that lay ahead for Rachel.

In addition to her relations with Bird, Rachel became involved with the Women's International League for Peace and Freedom (WILPF) whose mission occupied the same page with Rachel and Bird: WILPF envisioned a transformed world at peace, where there is racial, social, and economic justice for all people everywhere—a world in which:

- The needs of all people are met in a fair and equitable manner
- All people equally participate in making the decisions that affect them
- The interconnected web of life is acknowledged and celebrated in diverse ways and communities
- Human societies are designed and organized for sustainable existence (www.houstonpeacecamp.org)

Rachel studied hard; she knew her Concern would dovetail with any proclamation of nonviolence and peace.

In 1922 Rachel went to the Hague with the WILPF led by Jane Addams to explore and possibly execute changes in the Versailles Treaty which would hopefully lead to an avoidance of a new World War. She worked with the International Workers of the World (IWW). There were organizations that supported African Americans, Old Stock Americans, Europeans, and others like The Brotherhood of Sleeping Car Pullman Porters (*ATSM*, 51).

This was in 1923. With the blessing of the AFSC and Friends, Rachel left the AFSC and in 1924 returned to teaching at Woodbury, New Jersey junior and senior high school. She was as much a student as she was a teacher, and the time had come to blend the two identities into a solid strand and present it to students, who like her in childhood, were just beginning to experience the worlds of and outside their school, community, and their families. There was a world *out there* with troubles and trials as well as the beautiful, real, and good. As a student, Rachel was a sponge, absorbing information and looking at ways of communicating it. As a teacher, Rachel would release the contents of that sponge and spread it, as a part of her Concern across the student population in ways that were at once unique, functional, and in line with the teaching style of the day that was a combination of lecture and student recitation and interpretation.

While the year Rachel left the AFSC may have been a propitious time, all was not well with the world for those who wanted to make a better life in America, going back to the Johnson Act/Emergency Quota Act of 1921) in which "the law specified that no more than 3% of the total number of immigrants from any specific country already living in the United States in 1910 could migrate to America during any year." The Johnson Act morphed into the Immigration Act of 1924, signed into law by President Calvin Coolidge on 24 May 1924. First intended for the banning of Asian immigration, the bill extended into the lives of other culture groups, including Eastern Europeans (i.e. Jews and Slavs) and Southern Italians. The nation was nurturing a "Red Scare," concerning the feeling that these groups could not easily assimilate into American, white culture, and that they were taking jobs from the "real Americans" (http://immigrationtounitedstates.org).

Rachel was attuned to these developments in restricting those who wanted to make a new start in America (*ATSM*, 48). What she needed to do was figure out a way to encourage receptiveness toward cultural diversity at home so that the fear could be reduced, if not eliminated. Such a wish, embraced in her Concern, would be effectively supported by social scientists of all stripes, including folklorists, sociologists, and most of all, educators. It was time to "Resume Teaching" (*ATSM* 47).

Notes

1. These colleges were: Earlham (1847); Friends (1898); George Fox (1885); Guilford (1837); Haverford (1833); and Swarthmore (1864).
2. Transcripts, Bucknell University 1914.
3. See Chap. 8.
4. According to Free Job Descriptions: A bank examiner "conducts and directs the examination of state-chartered banks, their holding companies, subsidiaries, and affiliates…"
5. "Queries related to conduct are read regularly during the worship period when Friends put themselves through self-examination. The queries are a part of the Book of Discipline…" (Note from Rachel, *ATSM*, 27).
6. Christopher Harter 2018. *Founder's Day at Voorhees Normal and Industrial School*. Amistad Research Center.
7. The Rosenwald Fund (also known as the Rosenwald Foundation, the Julius Rosenwald Fund, and the Julius Rosenwald Foundation) was established in 1917 by Julius Rosenwald (1862–1932) and his family for "the well-being of mankind." Rosenwald became part-owner of Sears, Roebuck and Company in 1895, serving as its president from 1908 to 1922, and chairman of its board of directors until his death in 1932 (Wiki Accessed 10 May 2019).

References

Angell, Stephen, and Pink Dandelion, eds. 2018. *The Cambridge Companion to Quakerism*. Cambridge: Cambridge University Press.

Cavallo, Dominick. 1981. *Muscles and Morals: Organized Playgrounds and Urban Reform, 1880–1920*. Philadelphia: University of Pennsylvania Press.

DuBois, Rachel Davis. 1984. *All This and Something More: Pioneering in Intercultural Education*. Bryn Mawr: Dorrance.

Gulley, Philip. 2013. *Living the Quaker Way: Timeless Wisdom for a Better Life Today*. New York: Convergent Books.

Harter, Christopher. 2018. *Founder's Day at Voorhees Normal and Industrial School*. Amistad Research Center.

James, William. 1902. *The Varieties of Religious Experience*. New York: Modern Library Books, pp. 357–359.

Lemann, Nicholas. 2000. *The Big Test*. New York: Farrar, Strauss and Giroux.

CHAPTER 5

Development of Programs and a Career in Intercultural Education: The Assembly (1924–1929)

By 1923, Rachel contributed a great deal to the pacifist efforts of the American Friends Service Committee (AFSC) through her experience in the Deep South, the Women's International League for Peace and Freedom (WILPF), and the International Workers of the World (IWW). With the establishment of the Committee on Race Relations, she brought to fore, not only the knowledge of African Americans who participated in the "Great Migration" from plantation to factory, (Wilkerson 2010) but her concerns with the immigration policies of 1922 and 1924, as well which were designed to re-shape cultural focus, dynamic, and ultimately, history.

Rachel experienced a deep sense of purpose, and for her, the best spot for actualizing this depth was the classroom. She left the AFSC, and in 1924, she was hired to teach at Woodbury High School in Woodbury, New Jersey, not far from home in Woodstown and where she and Nathan lived in Pittman, New Jersey. She taught five freshman classes in social studies, her audience being primarily Caucasian. To fortify instruction, she used the teacher guides developed by Harold Rugg in 1923 (Rugg 1923) at Teacher's College at Columbia University. Rachel lets us know (*ATSM*, 47) that Rugg made a distinct mark on her presenting of social studies lessons in a variety of formats that led to a democratic society of choices.[1]

In addition to class work, Rachel and her colleagues were required to keep some kind of order during the weekly assembly programs.

It was the dismal once-a-week assembly programs I began to 'dream ahead' about. We teachers had to stand during the exercises to keep the pupils quiet. I thought to myself that we might have an outside speaker of prestige from each ethnic group in the school. In addition to making a formal presentation, we could ask each speaker to spend time visiting classes. I began to see how valuable this activity could be, not only for boosting the pride of minority students, but for all of us. (*ATSM*, 47)

She secured permission from the principal Mr. Thomas to install a new assembly format, and he allowed Rachel to do the assemblies for the next school year (1925), without reducing her class load.

For Rachel, the Assembly as she saw it, was her first chance in actualizing her Concern. She enlisted teachers in all of the subject areas (math, history, language, arts), students, and parents to help her out with designing the Assembly. The Assembly had three components:

(1) the *emotional*, guest assembly programs including music, drama, and oratory and an opportunity to see and hear stimulating representatives of various culture groups; (2) a *situational* approach offered smaller face-to-face group meetings and teas in which representative and students had the opportunity to meet and converse with interesting representatives of minority groups; and (3) an *intellectual* approach [consisted of] presentation in the homeroom and the classroom of an array of facts about the cultural heritages of the groups being studied and their contribution to American life. (DuBois 1940, 67)

The Assembly linked at least six actions.

1. An initial meeting where teachers invited members of the culture group to be presented. "Together teachers and guests discussed how misconceptions would be attacked in an indirect, but positive way. The guests gave the names of speakers and people of their group, talented in music, the dance, drama, and so on, who might be asked to be part of an assembly program."
2. Holding a meeting with the committee in charge of assembly programs (it was always urged that students be a part of this committee) … in which available talent was discussed and choices [for visitors] made.
3. Gathering students and staff together for the assembly—conducting the assembly.

4. Students and teachers study the culture groups presented, developing an informed mind of the program and its culture groups.
5. After the assembly, select students visited with members of the culture groups in an informal classroom setting for further, more intimate culture-sharing.
6. The students, now exposed to and informed about culture groups, could present a second assembly, presenting what they have learned in the assembly process (DuBois 1939).

The Assemblies were scheduled according to seasons and were well received, featuring the cultures of Germans (October), Italians, (December), African Americans (February), Jews (December) and so on. Rachel developed and gave students a pre-test and a post-test to determine if there was any change in attitude toward different peoples. She later used Neumann's *International Attitudes of High School Students, with Special Reference to Those Nearing Completion of Their High School Course* (1926). She found there *was change*, but one had to be careful not to substitute one being for another, thus avoiding stereotyping.

The Neumann scale was the first of its kind in measuring attitudes. It explored tendencies of persons to react positively or negatively to social situations, based on 12 attitudes: "Racialism, Nationalism, Imperialism, Militarism, Desire for Economic Prosperity, Tendency Toward Proletariat Cooperation for the Establishment of a World State, Public Opinion, Recognition of Rights of Other Nations and Peoples, Appreciation of the Worth of Other Nations and Peoples, International Cooperation, International Goodwill, and Humanitarian Attitudes" (Neumann 1926, 16–30).

Examples of Neumann's questionnaire statements asked respondents to address statements such as follows:

1. Anyone unwilling to salute the flag should either be deported or sent to prison (Neumann 1926, 102).
2. Weak or backward nations or peoples are so because they were born with poor brains (Neumann 1926, 105).

The only problem Rachel had to contend with was with the Assembly featuring African Americans held in February (*ATSM*, 55–57). The African American students were prepared to give a program on African American contributions to poetry and music. "The next morning, Mr. Thomas told me with a look of worry that we could not have the program because the Board of Education had objected the night before. ... A few days later Mr. Thomas told me that three men from the Board of Education would visit me in my home that night and ask me to resign because of a letter of complaint from the Woodbury American Legion" (*ATSM*, 56). She was visited, and the complaint was registered along with the request for her resignation. But Rachel had three things going for her. First, the Board members considered her an excellent teacher. Second, she had tenure and she could not be fired according to law, and three, she had no intention of resigning. There wasn't much anyone can do, and Rachel kept her job. The latter won overall. Rachel kept her job but didn't receive a raise in pay. The newspapers scorched her saying she was disloyal, that she believed in the "cult of nakedness [!]" (*ATSM*, 57). She was even doubted on her own ethnicity. It would not be the last time she experienced such venom. The African American program was canceled.

It is interesting how Rachel's Concern grew out of her experience in the Jim Crow South, but she didn't recognize racism in her own "northern" hometown. Tension between Whites and African Americans has never dissipated, *anywhere*. What the Woodbury Board of Education and the American Legion were so upset about can be linked to inherent racism, a feeling that African Americans were not capable of artistic expression *and* that they can't be trusted in interracial situations. They were a race, not a *culture*, and could not be trusted. Even with the stereotype of creativity dissolved, that issue of trust hangs heavy in the air today.

Despite the local outrage, the Assembly programs proceeded. Little did anyone know that they would become "viral" and other schools took interest in the Assembly and tried to emulate it.[2]

These three components, *emotion, intellect, and social*, formed the three basic elements of all of Rachel's works. Drawing first on popular social psychology, Rachel employed her intuition as well, believing that once students were exposed (emotion) to people of different culture groups, and heard *first hand* of these people's understandings of what their cultural practices contributed to life in America, they could explore (intellect) even further and mine the history as well as the culture of these groups. In providing a social outlet for understanding (social), be it by presenting their own assembly or engaging in a social situation, like a classroom visit with the representative, where the students could explore how these representatives impacted their views of culture groups or more about the culture groups through classroom activities with the culture bearer present.

These three approaches, emotional, situational, and intellectual, ebbed and flowed, shifting in focus. Rachel acknowledged this ebb and flow: "It is obvious that no hard and fast line can be drawn between these three approaches ... Although the emotional approach ... is uppermost in the dramatic assembly program, the situational approaches are also present; although the situational approach is predominant in the small group social situation, the emotional and intellectual approaches are also evident; and although the intellectual approach is used in the classroom, the emotional and situational approaches are by no means absent" (DuBois 1940, 67).

To dig deeper, the Assembly and Rachel's programs (to be discussed in Chap. 6) consisted of four sub-actions, each matching and guiding the three elements and their relationship with planning:

1. *Inform*: The gathering of information on culture groups and their contribution to American life
2. *Invite*: Engaging the skills and interests of students, teachers, parents, and community members in planning an assembly
3. *Include*: People in the actual programs
4. *Influence*: Exploring any changes in opinions about the culture group presented through the planning and execution of programs

These four "I's" supported the three elements of the Assembly. By involving others in design and execution the target of the program, in this case, the Assembly, students would have a hand in the creation of the program, giving them a sense of ownership, something they did not possess in the Assembly programs prior to Rachel's stepping in 1924/1925.

Given the time limit of the Assembly, participants got intensive presentations by the culture groups presented. To have meaning, the emotional aspect of the program *required* fleshing out, intellectually and socially. This further required further support from the teachers. As a result, the Assembly's elements had to come to life. Without teacher support, the objectives of the Assemblies would fail, their lack would be demonstrated by the guiding individual, the teacher, which would entirely defeat the purposes and functions of the programs, to sensitize and develop "cultural competence,"[3] tolerance, and sympathy for others.

The terms "tolerance" and "sympathy" refers to what Rachel hoped for with the assembly (and as you will see, this hope extended to all of Rachel's programs). To speak of "tolerance" and "sympathy" suggests a kind of "otherness" with those cultures presented in the Assembly. These were terms of the times, a plea to the emotional, suggesting that "others" were to be put up with or sympathized toward. I don't know if this is what Rachel meant. Yes, the culture groups presented in the Assembly, by virtue of their differences were to be recognized. But did Rachel suggest that people of difference had to be put up with or should be sympathized? On the one hand, these people were to be recognized for their "gifts" to life in America (Selig 2008). On the other hand, they were ordinary people like the students and teachers. Rachel, however, had a habit of singling people out and treating them for their "otherness." As we will see in Chap. 6, this singular approach by a singular soul came at a heavy cost threatening her Concern.

The style of teaching at the time continued to be lecture and recitation in which students memorized lessons and regurgitated their content (Cuban 1984). Given the nature of the Assembly, pedagogy had to change so that the support system of other informed classroom teachers would be included. Instead of memorization, there was *exploration*, joining the *me* as learner to *we* of an informed unit. This required a nimbleness on the part of the teacher who still had to toe the line of learning established by the school board but needed room to create mini learning communities in the classroom in order to relate emotion to intellect.

Rachel knew how to stay the course of the public-school system and was especially aware because she probably never left the critical eye of her dissenters. She engaged students in exploration while using the curriculum for all it could offer and changing what she could. She recognized the dramatic element in her work and was able to shape that to encourage the attributes of emotion, intellect, and sociability. The Assembly, as well as Rachel's other programs (to be explored in Chaps. 6 and 8), was structured like a play in three parts which revolved around the element of surprise found in the emotional approach of the assembly. Teachers, students, cultural representatives, parents, and residents were actors and audience in an all-inclusive endeavor toward the creation of what I call "a community of tolerance," a group of individuals who, although they might be different socially, historically, and economically, had the same goal, in this case, the development of meaningful relations and the creation of respect for others.

In terms of organization, the Assembly can be further divided into three parts, all of which incorporate the elements and the four "I's":

1. Preparation: Exploring preconceptions, selecting visitors, working with visitors and staff on production.
2. Presentation: Giving the Assembly—A Performance of Cultural Contributions
3. Review: Making sense out of the Presentation through Homeroom and/or Classroom activities.

This triptych given, what did an Assembly *look like*? The following description does not come from the Woodbury program. Rather, it comes from a description based on notes from the Service Bureau for Intercultural Education, which Rachel described in her EdD Dissertation, "Adventures in Intercultural Education" (1940. New York University) to be discussed in Chap. 6.

This Assembly featured African culture. This was the progression of the program (DuBois 1940, 75–76). It is presented in outline form in this particular reference; therefore, it is hard to get an actual feel for what happened:

1. Introduction: Miss Miriam Ephraim spoke on two exhibits on African art on display at New York City museums.
2. Address #1: Mr. Akintunde Dipeolu from Nigeria, West Africa: "African Youth at Home and Abroad."
3. Address #2: Mr. Caluza, "Zulu: African Music."
   a. Played three records to illustrate stages in the development of African music.
   b. Recited a poem extolling [a Zulu] chief.
   c. Showed how modern jazz has come directly from African rhythm.
4. Homeroom Discussion: Teacher presentation of facts about African history and culture.
5. Classroom Activities: Mr. Dipeolu spoke to five English classes, spending the whole day in the school. He spoke on African education in Africa, the work (both good and bad) of Christian missionaries, and the evolution of African languages and literature (there are about 160 dialects). He answered questions on music, art, and so on (DuBois 1940, 84).

The Assembly experience, from preparation to presentation to review was a highly choreographed program that didn't rush the emotional, intellectual, and the social. Students and culture representatives were able to work within whatever allotted class time they had and the assembly gathering time they had together. The students got to *know* over *knowing about*, which was what Rachel and her teammates wanted to achieve. With hope, participants, would come away enlightened and influenced by and encouraged to have a change of heart in recognizing the positive in immigrant presence in the home, community, nation, and perhaps the world.

1925–1928 was a banner period for Woodbury High; over 200 Assemblies presented! Rachel continued to use Neumann's International Attitudes scale to evaluate the Assembly, and found that through the instrument, there were shifts in attitudes among the students toward immigrant groups. Other schools had consulted Rachel on the nuts and bolts of putting on Assemblies, and there were still flakes of dissension among members of the school board and the American Legion (*ATSM*, 58). What was the problem here? Everyone wanted peace in the world. The Assembly was one way to promote it.

Given the success of the Assembly at Woodbury, Rachel wanted to make sure its design was secure. True to her belief in the scientific method which she learned of at Bucknell (see Chap. 4), Rachel decided to further her education. With Nathan's support, Rachel resigned from Woodbury and in 1929 was accepted into Teachers College's graduate program in Educational Sociology (*ATSM*, 61). Her resignation was bittersweet. The School Board and the American Legion were still skeptical about Rachel's allegiance to the United States, and Rachel was steadfast in the fact that she had tenure at Woodbury and would not resign her post. In making her resignation, these detractors might have heaved a sigh of relief. But Rachel's departure did not threaten the Assemblies, especially now that other schools were exploring them (*ATSM*, 62). Instead of dusting off her hands and saying, "it is finished," Rachel sought a stronger base to secure her work—graduate school. Before going into that experience, allow this "Tale from the Field" illustrate some of the parallels between Rachel's work and that of folklife in education.

Tale from the Field: Folk Arts in Education (FAIE)

My approach to school programs is similar to Rachel's in design and intent. I have been working in schools since 1980. My work has been mostly with 4th graders, except for two high schools, one public, the other private. My work has taken place in Arkansas, Florida, Indiana, Oklahoma,

Pennsylvania, and Texas. The programs were called "folk arts in education," or "FAIE" because they were funded in part by the Folk and Traditional Arts Program of the National Endowment for the Arts and by state and local arts agencies.

The steps to FAIE, as I put residencies together, are like the drama of emotion, intellect, and social of Rachel's programs, and the phases of Preparation, Presentation, and Review.

A FAIE program as I conduct it has many moving parts. Before actually going into a classroom, these are the preparatory steps that I as an FAIE practitioner follow: (1) fieldwork to identify individuals (tradition bearers) who practice a traditional art form and are willing to share with kids; (2) ascertaining from teachers and principals what they feel a program could do for the school, such as stemming bullying, harassment, and ultimately encourage students to be proud of their heritage; (3) select and suggest to principals who might be a good fit with the school found in the life and traditions of the school culture; (4) work with teachers to prepare a five- or ten-day calendar of topics which I present and link to the standards required by the state departments of education; (5) work with the tradition bearer on what he or she would like to do and could do in the classroom setting; and (6) observe the classes to be worked with to get a feel for student-teacher relations and teacher presentation. My preparatory work differs from Rachel's in that, first, in fieldwork; I don't seek out persons of "prestige" as Rachel did. The people I seek out are special but not in terms of education or social standing. I am interested in meeting people who are participants in some tradition, be it from making things to being a person from a traditional family with traditional expressions to share. I don't call them people of "prestige." They are *tradition bearers*, possessing and carrying forth the traditions of their homes and communities. For example, the children I have worked with met quilters, auctioneers, a woodworker, and a cowboy poet. All learned their skills through observation and imitation of elders, family, and community members, and were recognized for their for tradition and what they did. They were (and still are) ordinary people doing extraordinary things.

The teams Rachel worked with explored their misconceptions about various culture groups. This did not happen with FAIE. I would meet with the principals and teachers to learn about school needs, and I asked them *what they would like the program to do for them* (and this meant the students as well). I was often told about tensions between students of different cultures and how the program could possibly help in relieving bad feelings. Sometimes I was told that they would just like the students to feel better about themselves as they dealt with gang violence, drugs, and home disruption. I would ask the teachers and principals about who they would like to have visit their school and would suggest people who I had met through my fieldwork. Choices made, residency date (s)would be established, and I would contract the tradition bearers and work out a schedule of presentations, activities, and objectives for the teachers.

In addition to this, I would work with the tradition bearers, and we would work out a general outline of what they would like to do with the classes. This was shared with the teachers who would make suggestions on the presentations relating the class subject. These would be relayed to the tradition bearers, and the unit was set.

It's a long list, bringing an understanding of school culture together with the understanding of folk culture and bringing the two together to create a message of inclusion to the class. In the classroom there began steps to the presentation. Students are introduced to the vocabulary of folklore and descriptions (through hands-on activities) of how to learn about folklore and how it works for self and others. Over the course of the five- or ten-day program, I am a resident in the school, the one who works with the teacher to set the stage for the action to come.

But not all planning goes smoothly. Let me relate a "goof" caused by me not taking a school's culture into account:

> At one elementary school, I met with the principal to talk about needs and offer suggestions for visitors. This was when the FAIE project I was working on was a ten-day unit with two visitors instead of one. I asked her if the visitors could include an African American gospel sextet and a Japanese woman who mastered the traditional art of Japanese flower arrangement, *ikebana*. The White principal of this 98% African American school liked the idea of the gospel group, but with the *ikebana*, she sternly protested that this would not work for her students because they couldn't *identify* with it. The principal suggested that one of the best ways for me to "get" the culture of the school was to walk around the campus.
> Outside of the school walls, all seemed to look peaceful. But then I started walking around, paying attention to the grass; I found syringes, and there were those little plasticine bags that could have held drugs. The crowning blow was the scattering of spent gun shell casings. The experi-

ence was sobering and scary at best. I returned to the principal's office apologizing for not be more attentive to the school as a whole. We talked more about visiting tradition bearers and decided to invite an African American duo of deejay/rappers.

FAIE as I do it mirrors in part Intercultural Education as Rachel ultimately saw it: as a means by which to encourage social justice in a pluralistic world through tight and respectful coordination. While Rachel couldn't expect to convert the world around her to the world of tolerance, which she also referred to as "sympathy," the folklorist can't meet such a goal, either. But she had her hopes—and I had mine. In no way am I a "white knight on a white horse trying to save the people." And the only way there was to evaluate a program's effectiveness as I did it was through classroom review of the residency. Rachel, given her association with the scientific method, used another kind of qualitative analysis, a questionnaire of reactions to people of difference before and after a program.

We didn't do assemblies. I spent classroom periods about 40 to 50 minutes a session over a five or ten-day period. In the presentation, I talked with the students about folklife and what makes it so special—the learning process for the tradition bearer (Informing-Information), suggesting the student had folklife in their dealings with one another and others, giving them the opportunity throughout the residency to share their folklife and traditions. The presentations by the tradition bearers varied. A quilt maker talked about her grandmother and shared her quilts before she shared her quilt making (Math). A group of students huddled around a woodcarver as he explained how he carved a bird: carve all the wood away that didn't look like a bird (ART). A cowboy poet shared his poems, songs, and cattle brands (Music, Social Studies, and Language Arts). Each class was prompted to find out how the skills presented were traditional, by asking "the big Q:" how did the visitor learn the skill. The tradition bearers always engaged the students in an activity to reinforce the meeting. An auctioneer auctioned off school supplies and the students bid with Monopoly money. The quilters would let the students "take a stitch" in a quilt. The gospel group taught the students the parts of a song and they sang it together. After seeing slides of a pepper operation, students packed pepper crates brought to the classroom by a pepper farmer. The cowboy poet taught the students how to read cattle brands, and together they created both a brand for the class and a class cowboy poem.

One situation was particularly valuable. A principal told me that there were issues between the Haitian and non-Haitian students in the community that worried her. The Haitian population in that county was growing, and there were, on occasion, violent confrontations between Haitians and non-Haitians, sometimes due to drug running. I got permission from my Director to ask a Haitian storyteller from an adjacent county come to visit, and she shared stories about a character named Buki who was always getting in trouble. She encouraged the students to respond when the storyteller would shout "Crick!" If they wanted to hear a story, they would have to respond with "Crack!" One student kept asking her to translate Haitian phrases which she did until the last request. She firmly told the student she wouldn't translate it. For a moment, there was tension in the classroom. But then she got students to ask her for another story, and ill feelings subsided. She, like the others, knew what she was doing, and to a certain extent *why*. This was a county whose growth in the Haitian community was riddled with drugs and violence. There had to be a way of allaying the tensions, if just for a moment, and just with this particular group of students. When we reviewed the visit and the unit, we talked about how tensions could be relieved through traditions. Whether or not the students felt relief, and if they did, is hard to say. Folklorists working in education don't apply longitudinal studies of the effect of exploring tradition in the lives of those we supply in a residency (see Chap. 9).

As our sessions ended, I would be the one engaging students I would always ask the tradition bearer, "what does [your skill] mean to you?" There were no pat answers to this question, but there were some common feelings shared: love of the skill, respect for the people who shared it, feeling like a part of a community, and feelings of distraction from hard times.

With the Presentation phase completed, and the tradition bearer gone home, we moved into "Review" to go over and reinforce the lessons' objectives. Where Rachel promoted activities after the Assembly, FAIE review means going over what happened in the residency and how it related to folklife. FAIE activities are built into the Presentation phase.

Like Rachel, the work of the folklorist in the schools requires the wearing of different hats and the ability to utilize those hats at any given moment. It requires a certain amount of trust that we can do this, but nothing will work without the participation of the teacher, principal, the visiting tradition bearer, and sound but flexible planning. The teacher is at once guide, savior, and example. His or her part in the program, just as it was for the teachers Rachel worked with, is hyper-essential. With folklife education, we hope for the same.

Notes

1. Rachel is referring to a series of Social Studies pamphlets created by Harold Rugg, including "Americanizing Our Foreign Born," published before 1923. Rugg was on the education faculty at Teachers College (Columbia University) and published extensively on the relationship between children and schooling.
2. Rachel learned of this when she began her graduate studies. See Chap. 6.
3. "Cultural Competence" is a term used to describe the ability to understand cultural diversity without compromising one's own culture.

References

Cuban, Larry. 1984. *How Teachers Taught: Constancy and Change in American Classrooms, 1890–1980*. New York, London: Longman.

DuBois, Rachel Davis. 1939. "Peace and Intercultural Education." *The Journal of Educational Sociology* 12 (7): 418–424.

———. 1940. *Adventures in Intercultural Education*. EdD diss., New York University.

———. 1984. *(ATSM) All This and Something More: Pioneering in Intercultural Education*. Bryn Mawr: Dorrance.

Neumann, George B. 1926. *A Study of International Attitudes of High School Students*. New York: Teachers College, Columbia University.

Rugg, Harold. 1923. *The Social Studies Pamphlets*. New York: BiblioLife.

Selig, Diana. 2008. *Americans All: The Cultural Gifts Movement*. Cambridge: Harvard University Press.

Wilkerson, Isabel. 2010. *The Warmth of Other Suns: The Epic Story of America's Great Migration*. New York: Vintage.

CHAPTER 6

Graduate School and the Service Bureau for Intercultural Education (1929–1940)

As I presented in Chap. 5, Rachel began to come of age as both a professional and an advocate for cultural diversity through the creation of the Assembly at Woodbury Junior/High School. In constructing the Assembly, Rachel developed a three-pronged approach for planning and execution: (1) the appeal to the *emotional*, a direct application to the senses through an introduction of a culture-bearer who addressed the Assembly about his or her culture and its contributions to American life; (2) the encouragement of *intellect*, classroom explorations of the history, and culture of the culture group presented in the Assembly; and (3) a *social* component, in the form of students offering their own interpretation of the Assembly, or an opportunity to visit with the culture-bearer in a social setting.

Rachel and her Assembly advisory team provided colleagues with information on the culture groups featured in the Assemblies and their contributions to American life. The plan was to *inform, involve, invite*, and *influence* participation in the Assembly experience. To make sure they were on the right track, Rachel tested the students on their beliefs past and present regarding culture groups. The programs ran through a combination of dramaturgy, intuition, and a smattering of common sense. Up until then, the Assembly she wanted more, she wanted to ensure the success of the Assembly as a replicable event. To do this, Rachel felt the need to gain further training and experience with testing. To make this happen, she left Woodbury in 1929 and registered at Teacher's College/Columbia

© The Author(s) 2019
J. Rosenberg, *Intercultural Education, Folklore, and the Pedagogical Thought of Rachel Davis DuBois*,
https://doi.org/10.1007/978-3-030-26222-8_6

University's program in Educational Sociology (1929–1937) and then to New York University's same program, 1937–1940, where she completed her EdD.

At this juncture in her life, Rachel was perhaps more determined than ever to create a usable program that could contribute to the eradication of racism and the promotion of justice. And it was through the early 1930s and her initial graduate school experiences at Teachers College (TC) and New York University (NYU) that Rachel found support, assistance, and collegiality like she had never experienced before.

This chapter explores the longest clip in Rachel's *longue durée*, ten years, reflecting mountains of glory and valleys of misery. The following covers six powerful overlapping moments in Rachel's life: (1) her graduate school training; (2) the creation of the Service Bureau for Intercultural Education (SBIE); (3) The Service Bureau and the Progressive Education Association (PEA); (4) the development of the Group Conversation Method and the Neighborhood-Home Festival; (5) the Americans All-Immigrants All radio series of 1938–1939; and (6) Rachel's resignation from the Service Bureau.

At Teachers College, Rachel was mentored by a host of progressive educators including Daniel R. Kulp II, William Heard Kilpatrick, and Harold Rugg. From them she received and developed a "tool kit" for her work, measuring the efficacy of the Assembly.

As a student at Teacher's College, Rachel's advisor was Daniel R. Kulp II (1888–1980) (*ATSM*, 63). He presented the field of Educational Sociology, based, in part of Durkheimian thought that the school is a "practical agency whereby the child is inducted into and made acquainted with the character and meanings of his own community culture" (Durkheim 1956, 11).

Kulp taught: "An attitude is a tendency to move toward or away from a value, so we have negative and positive attitudes. To change the attitude, you change the value" (*ATSM*, 63). This is a simple extrapolation of thought by Rachel. Kulp broke this statement out in the following manner in such a way that one can see attitudinal development as just that, a *process of living*.

Kulp starts out with *habit*: "forms of behavior whose characteristics in reoccurrence are sufficiently alike to be recognizable. They are the stable, persistent, continuous behaviors of a personality" (1932, 208). Out of habits, *wishes* are born, "instincts revamped by institutions (church, home, school). They are formulations in logic (by words) of behavior in an imagined social situation" (1932, 159). The four wishes, originally supplied by W. I. Thomas (1921/1971, 27–28), are (1) the wish for recognition; (2) the wish for response; (3) the wish for new experience; and (4) the wish for safety. In later days a fifth wish was created: the wish for new experience outside of the self (Kulp 1932, 159).

Turning to "attitude," Kulp defined it as the combination of habits and wishes: "Wishes differ from habits in that they arise when habits are insufficient. They are the inventive and creative processes of behavior. ... Collectively, habits are institutions [and] wishes are changes. ... The struggles between conventionality and personality are the struggle between habits and wishes" (Kulp 1932, 152).

Thus, habit + wish = attitude—a basic equation.

For Rachel, what did she want to change through the Assembly? Kulp's teaching meshed well with the three elements that guided the Assembly—emotion, intellect, and social—and the five wishes. Rachel took the three elements and five wishes to heart, and she built them into her MA research, examining the structure and success (or failure) of the Assembly in 15 schools on the eastern seaboard and 1 school in San Francisco. As she had, before registering at TC, Rachel applied Neumann's Attitudinal Scale as her analytic instrument indicating shifts in student attitude. She hoped to overcome habit with the introduction of the benefits of the wishes which would encourage shifts in attitudes.

With her love of the framework of the scientific method and understanding of habits, wishes, and attitudes, Rachel was able to create and experiment, first, on the Assembly. For example, the application could have looked like this:

Hypothesis: Attitudes can be changed from negative to positive
Experiment: (1) Plan, present Assembly
Evaluate: Through written and spoken comments about the Assembly, along with statistical information provided through Neumann, evaluate an Assembly program: through anecdotal and statistical information.

This is what Rachel did: she identified 15 schools on the east coast and 1 in San Francisco. She trained committees to do the Assemblies at their schools and evaluate their success according to her hypothesis. She presented her findings in her EdD dissertation, "Adventures in Intercultural Education" (1940. New York University). Her expert-sounding writing suggests the experiment was a success.

Rachel published her project work primarily in the Quaker journal, *The Friends Intelligencer* some in *The Journal of Educational Sociology*. In her 1930 article, "Measuring Attitudes," she echoed Kulp's teachings by writing, "Not only can attitudes be measured, but they can be scientifically modified or built, not by magic, but by intelligent control of the means.... Attitudes are habits of the mind, mind sets. Our social environment determines our attitudes as the air determines our breathing" (*ATSM*, 1930, 467–468).

Rachel's 1932 piece, "Shall We Emotionalize Our Students," tells us that IQ, EQ (Emotion Quotient), and SQ (Social Quotient) must work in concert for there to be attitude adjustment. While the EQ and SQ might be more difficult to quantify, they can be qualitatively explored and viewed alongside IQ, which, in respect is also hard to quantify because it is not a stable measure (Lemann 2000).

By 1933 the Assembly plan (now called the Woodbury Unified Assembly Plan) was near completion for Rachel's MA degree. Kulp sent Rachel to schools in New York and Englewood, Cliffs, New Jersey, to train teachers in the philosophy and nuts and bolts of the Assembly. As she did this, she also sought out possible venues and contacts that might have had a longer-term relationship for program execution. One such contact was Everett Clinchy (1897–1986), a Presbyterian minister who founded the National Conference of Christians and Jews in 1928. His efforts gave Rachel a boost into what became the Service Bureau for Intercultural Education (SBIE), first by allowing the use the Conference office equipment to copy reading and resource materials for educators, and second by coordinating opportunities for Rachel to describe the work she was doing at TC to interested parties.

In 1933, Clinchy organized the first of two conferences where Rachel expressed the opinion that the works of cultural anthropologists Franz Boas and Ruth Benedict were to be applauded, as they attempted bringing social healing and recognition to Rachel's works through their work in cultural anthropology and its focus on peoples' whole culture and expression.

In the audience was Teresa Mayer Durlach who was interested in intercultural work, primarily with the Englewood schools. That led her to have her friend, Jacob Weinstein, to offer a gift of $5000 from the American Jewish Committee (AJC) (*ATSM*, 66). Rachel easily reported to Weinstein what she would do with the gift. She would hire two of the Englewood teachers to work with her to conduct and to test on 15 Assemblies in the Metropolitan New York City schools, supplemented by her fee for teaching courses on Intercultural Education at NYU. At the time, Rachel did not know that these funds were to be provided by the American Jewish Committee (AJC), founded in 1906 for the global support of Jewish civil rights, "to prevent the infraction of the civil and religious rights of Jews, in any part of the world … and to render all lawful assistance to Jews whose rights were threatened." When she found this out, she must have been doubly pleased, as she was given funds by an organization whose culture fascinated her.[1]

For further guidance on how to "stretch out" the gift, Rachel approached Dr. Mabel Carney who specialized in rural and African American cultures. Carney told Rachel that the Works Progress Administration (WPA) had available funding that she could use, but the record does not indicate just how much funding Rachel used, and Rachel did not record their welcomed efforts.

The second conference Clinchy organized took place in 1934. He invited people he felt would be interested in Rachel's work(s) to a luncheon at New York City's Town Hall Club (*ATSM*, 66). Rachel spoke to the Woodbury Plan in Englewood and Washington, DC. The response to her talk was favorable, and representatives from the Progressive Education Association (PEA) who attended the luncheon further scrutinized Rachel's work and invited her to work under the auspices of the PEA. The relationship was formed, and since the PEA had a commission on human relationships, it christened Rachel's work under the new Commission on Intercultural Education. For the PEA, forging this relationship was a part of the Association's efforts at recasting and developing its identity as an answer to social need and cause for cohesion (Graham 1967). Fortunately, the Service Bureau kept up its work despite PEA activity. And in the long run, Rachel's goal of progressive works and identification with social justice as she saw it ran counter to the dispassionate elitism of the PEA.

What was the PEA? The organization, known as The Association for the Advancement of Progressive Education, was founded in April 1919 by educator Stanwood Cobb (1881–1982), who was disillusioned with his teaching post at the US Naval Academy. He chanced to hear a lecture by Marietta Johnson, founder of the Organic School at Fairhope, Alabama, founded in 1907, and he was inspired by her naturalistic approach to education, where students were unfettered by traditional pedagogy and were allowed to pursue interests, guided by their teachers. It was a naturalistic education, in which students were divided by life stages: four- and five-year-olds were in kindergarten, six- and seven-year-olds in the "first life" class, and so on. High school students attended their school after those in the "fourth life," "12- and 13-year olds" (Newman, in Sadivnik and Semel, 2002, 28).

Most of the association's first members were laymen. This was thought to be a positive thing, given that the membership's strength in numbers would call out the need professional educators and politicians alike for the organization to advance. The membership listed two sets of aims. The first set of aims focused on what the Association would provide:

1. To propagate the principles of progressive education by means of
   a. A periodical publication to serve as the official organ of the Association, issued free to all members
   b. Newspaper and magazine articles
   c. Lectures
2. To influence public education toward progressivism by educating the public to demand it
3. To be of service to laymen and educators through
   a. An exchange bureau
   b. Counseling and cooperating with parents in solving their educational problems
   c. Encouraging the training of teachers in the principles and methods of progressive education
   d. Giving field aid to those who are organizing or developing progressive schools (Graham 1967, 28)

The Association would provide the child with the following attitudes:

1. The freedom to develop naturally
2. Interest, the motive of all work
3. The Teacher a Guide, Not a Task-Master
4. Scientific study of pupil development
5. Greater attention to all that affects the child's physical development
6. Cooperation between school and home to meet the needs of child-life
7. The progressive school a leader in Educational movements (Graham 1967, 29–30).

The Association changed its name in 1931 to the Progressive Education Association (Graham 1967). The organization did not ascribe to any one approach; instead, it served to advocate numerous approaches. On one side of the spectrum, a school could use progressive principles for scientific explorations (Cremin 1961). On the other side of the arch, a school could promote learning through play (Pratt 1948/1970) and a sense of child development as moral and playful as well as scientific (deLima 1926; Mitchell 1953). The point to the entire enterprise was that as long as the focus remained on the child, no program was right, nor was one program wrong.

Though the PEA didn't have much to do with immigrant studies, members during the 1930s were thinking that the 1930s was some kind of "age of ethnicity," and it might be useful to associate itself with organization(s) that promoted the ethnic side of progressive education. In this respect, the Service Bureau for Intercultural Education was one such organization. It may have been a kind of Hail Mary pass for the PEA.[2]

But the PEA forged ahead in its allegiance to Rachel's programs. In 1935, the PEA journal, *Progressive Education*, published 14 articles on aspects of intercultural education, including Rachel's article, "Our Enemy—the Stereotype" (1935, 145–150), which called for an approach to society and humanity not as interchangeable boxes loaded with preconceptions, but (1) minus the box and (2) a recognition of diversity that makes the world what it is.

In the 1930s, the PEA focus on ethnicity was more a desire for assimilation than cultural inclusivity. In actuality, the PEA was not altogether supportive of Rachel's work after 1937. She did not preach assimilation. She wanted people to see the power of tradition in immigrant lives and how it contributed to the sustenance of American life. She didn't treat cultural diversity as a large whole of humanity as the PEA saw it. She saw individual diversity contributing to the whole, and to see how that was the case, information on immigrant groups had to focus on who they were and how they contributed to the national fabric. She promoted blending without disappearing, and this was completely counter to the PEA who was hoping for professional legitimacy and public approval in education through the evaporation of cultural singularity. But Rachel saw it this way: if there were no immigrants (read "ethnic"), there would be no America (1936).

The Service Bureau could not serve the PEA, and the PEA could not serve the Bureau. The relationship came to a head amid Rachel's claim that Judaism was a culture, and it was met with hostility by a member of the AJC who was active in the PEA who countered saying Judaism was a religion only.

What was Judaism that interested Rachel at the time? Was it a religion? Was it a culture? This was one area of cultural diversity that brought up great conflict. Why? It stems from the beliefs beyond the Shema, the basic belief symbolizing Judaism: "Hear, O Israel: the Lord Our God is One Lord" (Deuteronomy 6:14, JPS). Rachel's interest and understanding of Judaism came from one rabbi, Mordechai Kaplan (1881–1993) who, founded, with his son in-law Ira Eisenstein, what can be called America's Judaism, *Reconstructionism*. In his 1934 masterpiece *Judaism as a Civilization* Kaplan wrote: "The Jew's religion is but one element in his life that is challenged by the present environment" (1934, 177). Jews possess a kind of "otherness," a sense of being that is not isolated, but is detached from the mainstream religions: "Judaism as otherness is … something far more comprehensive than Jewish religion. It includes that nexus of a history, literature, language, social organization, folk sanctions, standards of conduct, social and spiritual, ideas, esthetic values, which in their totality form a civilization" (1934, 178). Judaism is a way of being with infinite components. It does not begin with Deuteronomy and it does not end with the end of the High Holy days of the Day of Atonement. One *breathes Judaism, but one doesn't condemn the Other*. We are all hyphenated in one way or another, and there must be room for that (DuBois 1936).

This didn't sit well for even the Jews in Rachel's midst were of the most liberal of thought, the Reform, and a line was drawn in the sand. Reform Jews have been able to survive because it is a relatively non-confrontational set of practices. A mid- to late nineteenth-century phenomenon, Reform Judaism was created from Western European desire not to disturb the Christian *status quo*. Its worship was in English, the High Holidays of Rosh Hashana and Yom Kippur were probably the only activities that set them apart from the mainstream Protestants and the Catholics. With the approach of Eastern European Jews, worry did set in due to the facts of language (Yiddish over English), dress, and foodways. It was enough of a perceived threat to American identity that the 1924 Reed-Johnson Immigration Act put a virtual halt on Jewish life outside of Western Europe. But in the 1930s, with the fear of Nazism and other forms of radical nationalism, people had to act. And it was not through Reconstructionism. It was risky, it was different. But it was something Rachel identified with, perhaps because of the concept of civilization, but also because Quakers were thought of in their own communities and outside them as being Separate, being in the world and out of it at the same time (Hamm 2003).

With passion and commitment, Rachel/the Bureau continued in her works, amassing and sharing resources on ethnic group contributions to American life, conducting Assembly trainings, and teaching at NYU. It was a time of great concern for history and culture with the specter of Nazism and xenophobia. Rachel's classes recognized this turn of events and questioned how could they reach adults. She reminded her students of one of the premises of Educational Sociology is that "adults do not act according to what they know, but according to how they feel about what they know." She further suggested they needed to reach emotion in a positive way, "drawing from her experience of the three elements and five wishes first promoted in the Assembly" (*ATSM*, 83).

Rachel suggested that her classes experiment on themselves, by coming to her apartment and to bring friends of different ethnic and religious and national backgrounds. She asked dancer Dvora Lapson and music teacher Wallace House who knew folksongs to attend this particular gathering. According to Rachel, approximately 35 people gathered to join in what Rachel called "Group Conversation" (Crispin 1987).

George Crispin's Temple University dissertation "Rachel Davis DuBois: Founder of the Group Conversation as an Adult Facilitator for Reducing Intercultural Strife" (1987) used oral history interviews with Rachel and her colleagues to explore Group Conversation: "the face to face sharing of experiences both of the past and of the present in a spontaneous atmosphere which quickly produces rapport. This kind of sharing helps to break down the fears and differences of age, race, ethnicity, or class as liabilities" (Crispin 1987, 6).

Group Conversation was a method, a way of getting from the skepticism inherent in intolerance to the embracing nature of tolerance. Rachel facilitated these talks by introducing herself and sharing some of her South New Jersey Quaker heritage. She then asked the group to share something about themselves and would then launch into a topic, such as holidays, childhood games, and "red letter days"—days of some importance to the participants. Once the group began talking, Rachel would position herself in a corner to watch the talk and make notes about how participants acted during the conversation. When conversation slowed down, she would reenter the conversation and ask the talkers what they thought about what they had just done—she asked for participant evaluation. One participant said, "I think we have found a new way of coming together." Another, a doubter claimed, "You did it tonight, but I don't think you'll be able to do it again" (Crispin 1987, 24).

Group conversations took place in winter and spring, seasonally, around religious holidays. Primarily a group of Christians and Jews, the participant evaluations remained in the positive. Basically, Group Conversation worked, and it became the basis for its intensified sister, the Neighborhood-Home Festival.

The Neighborhood-Home Festival came into being around 1937—an exact date is not recorded.[3] Rachel wrote about it prior to 1941 as she described the program to a new-found friend at a workshop to be considered in the next chapter. Rachel writes in her guide, *Get Together Americans: Friendly Approaches to Racial and Cultural Conflicts Through the Neighborhood-Home Festival* (1943, herein called *GTA*). "The Neighborhood-Home Festival is what happen when a group of people, culturally as mixed as is the community in which it meets, come together for relaxation; when those people converse, as a group on universal themes related to a season, a significant event, or an idea and find realization and expression of their common humanity" (*GTA*, 3).

The festival is not a festival in the traditional sense of the word. It is not a display of actions, a performance, like dance or crafts, but it is more of a psychosocial event that brings people in to be a part of a community in the making. "The welfare of the group ... whether it be the family, community, nation, or the world itself, is based on the development of healthy, integrated personalities able to transcend their egocentric selves and to merge, in a creative way, into the whole. This means finding ways to share unique qualities and differences" (*GTA*, 5).

The Festival was not intended as a therapy group either, although the experience could be therapeutic. Rather, Rachel saw it as an example of *cultural democracy—the creative use of difference*. "Democracy is an atmosphere in which this can happen, whether between individuals, within families, among groups in a country, or among countries" (*GTA*, 5).

As she did with the Assembly, the Neighborhood-Home Festival was coordinated as a drama in three acts: (1) conversation; (2) the festival proper; and (3) a party. The idea was to talk about a subject first, engage in some traditional behaviors that reinforced the subject of the talk, second, and last have a party where conversation and tradition met in less formal circumstances. For example, the group would talk about holiday celebrations and then engage in a Saint Lucia festive tradition consisting of lighting a crown festooned with candles. The talk would center around the tradition and its importance, and after the group would gather informally around food and drink to share more about holidays or whatever else the participants wanted to talk about in small groups.

It sounds like a very loose affair, but true to Rachel's thinking, it wasn't. The four "I's" were thoroughly engaged, and the event was tightly orchestrated. There were coordinators who had to identify potential participants from various culture groups, learn about the cultures to be present, and invite the people to the event (inform, involve, invite). There were coordinators who arranged the festival space, and there were coordinators in charge of the food. The people who came to the Festival were almost handpicked for the event, and all coordinators were cautioned about behaviors and speech. An old-stock American presence was required. Coordinators during the conversation had to make sure derogatory names weren't applied to African Americans (like "darky"). Jewish participants had to be steered away from talking about their history and into talk about celebrations (*GTA*, 72). Influence would come about as the conversation, and activity drew to a close, and the party would begin. Influence was anecdotal. The festival did not have the feel for formal testing, nor was it applied.

The Neighborhood-Home Festival was an educational experience that served several functions. It was an *art form*, a celebration of people's music, song, dance, and art. The event was a form of *social interaction* feeding the five wishes for experience, recognition, response, and experience beyond the self in a safe environment. And again, while the festive occasion was not a therapy session, it did *aid to the release of tensions* (*GTA*, 91–120).

The Neighborhood-Home Festival grew out of the Group Conversation method, but Group Conversation was not an isolated form. Since it could take place anywhere at any time, it was a portable activity. The methods of Group Conversation and the Neighborhood-Home Festival are, in Rachel's words, "difficult to describe because [they] are an emotional experience and needs to be felt in order to be understood" (1946, 557). They are examples of the emotion quotient and the social quotient in action and are examples of intercultural education as a moving force.

As Group Conversation and the Neighborhood-Home Festival carried on, Kulp left Teachers College in 1937. Rachel transferred to study full time at New York University. She studied Educational Sociology under Frederick Thrasher, a colleague of Kulp's. Money was tight, and soon financial support of her classes was suspended.

In 1938 Rachel couldn't understand this turn of events, but soon she found she had other fish to fry. In 1938, CBS radio invited Rachel to guide a series of programs on the contributions to American life by culture groups. The program "Americans All-Immigrants All" aired between 1938 and 1939. It was, in effect, Rachel's "swan song," as the Service Bureau for Intercultural Education (which was named after the PEA left the scene) felt its work would be better suited for a man to direct. Additionally, the Service Bureau board felt Rachel was overzealous in her work and didn't possess leadership qualities. As a result, this woman who founded and directed the Bureau for almost five years was demoted from Director to Researcher (*ATSM*, 92–93).

Americans All-Immigrants All was a product of the United States Department of the Interior, Office of Education, and the Columbia Broadcasting System with "the cooperation of the Service Bureau for Intercultural Education and assisted by the Works Progress Administration." It differed from the American School of the Air (ASA), established by William Paley in 1930, in that the ASA was broadcast in the classroom, and the Americans All series broadcast at home on the weekends. Their benefits, according to William Bianchi (2008), however, were quite similar. The ASA and Americans All programs: (1) exposed students to world figures; (2) stimulated the imagination using drama, music, and sound; (3) reunited "home and school in the educational process; and (4) deemphasized drill and practice." According to the staff of Americans All, the "programs are designed to promote a more appreciative understanding of our growing American culture through the dramatization of the contributions made by the many groups which are a part of it" (Americans All flyer, ca. 1938). The radio series consisted of 26 programs, aired 13 November 1938 through May 1939, 2:00, Eastern time, 1:00 Central time, and 11:00 Pacific time. The series production was highly dramatized, giving the listener a sense of what it was like for the people and sounds featured in the Series. The series attempted to answer the questions of: What brought people to this country from the four corners of the earth? What gifts did they bear? What were their problems? What problems remain unsolved? The programs highlighted contributions to American life by Germans, Scandinavians, Hispanics, Italians, and African Americans. The dramatizations also addressed issues of immigration, industry, arts, and craft.

"Americans All—Immigrants All. This is the story of how you, the people of the United States, you and your neighbors, your parents and theirs, were the most spectacular movement in all recorded time. The movement of millions of men, women, and children from other lands to the land they made their own. It is a story of what they endured and accomplished, and it is also the story of what this country did for them."[4]

Materials relating to the featured groups were made available to the public, including schools. In addition, there was broadcast a plea for tolerance at the end of the program: "Tolerance, what is it? Why is it top-column news today? Tolerance is just understanding the other fellow, but in a democracy we need more. We need an appreciation for having in our midst people of many backgrounds who have contributed to much that is essential to our happiness and well—being."[5] In her EdD dissertation "Adventures in Intercultural Education" (1940), Rachel made numerous suggestions as to what radio program would feature what. The recordings were made available on phonographic disks that could be obtained for educational purposes outside of the Sunday time slot. For those who listened to the broadcasts from home, they were surrounded by technology together, engaged in a cultural fireside chat, emphasized by President Franklin Roosevelt as a series that "would make more significant the human struggle to achieve our freedom as safeguarded by our Constitution; the values of inter-American understanding and friendship, and the processes of building a finer and more enduring American culture by developing a greater appreciation of the rich heritages that have come to us through the many races and nationalities which make up our population" (Government Printing Office 1939).

Even though the Series received the Women's National Radio Committee award for 1938–1939, the new SBIE Board still wanted Rachel to be out of the way, as far away as physically possible. The Board members even suggested she move to California to coordinate her programs. Rachel refused. She would always be a child of the agrarian east. This was an example of unadulterated misogynist thinking against her gender, mission, and strengths. There were others involved with the Service Bureau who resigned in support of her.[6] They "got it" in terms of her Concern and path toward meeting it head-on at all costs through varieties of education. That Concern was Rachel's keystone, holding fast her faith, practice, and professionalism. No one was going to get rid of her. But in the name of sanity, she had to act, and doing this, she did by involuntarily resigning from the Service Bureau, in 1940, leaving it in the dust of its own prejudices.

Tale from the Field: Group Conversation in Use with Nurses and Their Hospital

How can nurses contribute to the cultural and corporate welfare of a hospital while holding on to the mission of modern-day nursing first articulated by Florence Nightingale (*Wikipedia*, accessed 29 May 2019) and was incorporated into the American Nursing Association (ANA) Code of Ethics for nurses practiced today? Key elements in the Code relate to relationships with patients and employers, highlighting respect, dignity, and professionalism. Sometimes it is difficult to bring all of this together, often because there are *kinds* of staff competing for different kinds of well-being. Nurses want to know: how can I best serve the client and by extension, the hospital as a blessing and corporate monument to health? This, too, is a question of intercultural blending.

I was asked by nurses at a hospital in Kentucky to address these sorts of questions. The large question was, "how can we get along?" The question was asked by nurses who wanted to improve relations with hospital administration because they felt as if there was a gap between them caused by the latter's concern with financial health and the former's dedication to patient health. The workshop was spearheaded by the nurses, and I don't know if they reached out to the administration to attend. Planning was simple for me because the nurses took it upon themselves to arrange for a meeting space and marshaling the nurses for participation, for which they received certification credit.

To meet the question head-on, I realize I adapted Rachel's method of Group Conversation. The group I was working with, however, weren't strangers. Most of them knew one another. So, in addition to asking first about experiences with holidays and the like, I also posed different, perhaps, more direct questions on the emotional front through a group activity where the nurses, already separated by tables, would employ a spinner device which at each point on a circle, the pointer for the device would land and the spinner would discuss with her groups such questions as "recall the first time you were being stereotyped" and "talk about the first time you stereotyped someone because you felt they were odd or different." We talked about occasions when they felt different from others, in addition to the ways the nurses treated patients and physicians. This was our starting point. From there we talked about life's work and what were some of the best ways of acknowledging difference without compromising identities as professional nurses. In discussion, one person at each table was a scribe, taking in the talk and keeping a running record of topics, discussion, and reaction. By the end of the 2 ½ hour session, some participants said they had a clearer way of working closer together as a team, enhancing their position as professionals engaged in the medical and social well-being of patients. The workshop might not have shed any new light on the situation. Rather, it was more of an affirming experience through which one could get in-service points.

Tale from the Field: The Mental Health Center: Group Conversation Among 200 and Thinking on the Fly

I was asked to conduct an in-service program on cultural awareness for a mental health center in Oklahoma City. The goal of the program was to provide opportunities for staff to heighten awareness in its interactions with a multicultural clientele. After consulting with staff and administration, I decided that a conversational approach would be useful. Approximately 200 people attended the in-service program, and I felt that there could be small group discussions that would last 15 minutes and that after discussions came to a close, the large group would contribute its thoughts and feelings as we would create a structure for meeting their goals.

Most participants in this one-day program were social workers whose professional goal is to serve social groups and individuals with resources to meet and dissolve conflict. The center's mission is "[t]o positively change the lives of youth and adults by providing and coordinating their behavioral and physical health in an effort to strengthen families and support the community" (Organization handbook). Much of the planning for this particular program was conducted over the phone, and it also required permission from my employer to take the time off to conduct the workshop.

According to the National Association of Social Workers Code of Ethics, "the primary mission of the social work profession is to enhance human well-being and help meet the basic human needs of all people, with particular attention to the needs and empowerment of people who are vulnerable, oppressed, and living in poverty. A historic and defining feature of social work is the profession's focus on individual well-being in a social context and the well-being of society. Fundamental to social work is the attention to the environmental forces that create, contribute to, and address problems in living" (NASW, 2016 https://www.socialworkers.

org/About/Ethics/Code-of-Ethics-English). The social worker, in order to do his or her job, is to be nimble and knowledgeable about the people and the cultures they work with. Such was the case with this Center, and apparently, there were a lot of mixed feelings when it came to learning about and incorporating client culture into the work.

As I think about how I conducted the workshop, I again find myself hearkening back to Rachel's program in Group Conversation. Although many of the people in this workshop knew one another, too, there were things they did not know, and through conversation, we explored those unknowns, such as their experiences of positive and negative encounters with clients, and how they could put such experiences to use when working with clients. We talked about ranges of behavior—body language, tone of voice, and the many ways one could approach a client. The group decided these were defining factors in its work, and that it was essentially its responsibility to craft respect for clients as the group knew them: as human beings in need of support.

There was one subject that came up that I was not prepared for, and this was how to deal with the tensions between the clinical staff and the clerical workers. There was consternation over how each group treated each other, and there seemed to be no answers to be found. To explore this, the workshop participants once again turned to each other to identify what it was that was breeding the tension. And as Rachel would work it out, we returned to the concept of values and attitudes, how they were expressed, and how to act with and on them. There were issues of tone of voice, of what looked like one was not paying attention to the other, and an overall feeling of disrespect. As we talked about this, I asked how the clinicians felt about the clerical workers, and many responded that they saw the "clericals" as being somewhat below the "clinicals." How to fix it? The consensus was to work on changing attitudes by talking up these feelings as they arose. There was, in my estimation, no singular fix. But we made a start, and from the written evaluations of the in-service, the participants felt they could begin to work together to create their own respectful culture, paying attention to tone of voice, choice of words, body language, and time management in a confined environment, the center.

From graduate school and into the world, these were Rachel's moments on what started to be a joyful climb to a mountain top with a great view of the woods below. At Woodbury, the seeds were planted. Teachers College and NYU saw to it that those seeds were nurtured. With the Service Bureau and the PEA, the view was in constant storm conditions. Moving forward, the next chapters tell of how Rachel weathered the storm.

NOTES

1. From "Jewish Learning" AJC information page accessed from the AJC information page, accessed 11 March 2019.
2. I write here from personal experience with a PEA school. I felt that the school, while presenting itself to the public as an opportunity for individual expression, it promoted it as long as one behaved within its self-defined system. We were tested, we were categorized by our academic test scores, and I know, for myself, I was closely watched in my social development. In fact, soon after I graduated, a teacher friend and I went through my file and discarded many of the teachers' and administrators' notes on me. Also, the school experience, while it did allow a certain amount of latitude, personally, it made me yearn to attend a large university where I wouldn't be watched so closely. Ah, "even paranoids have enemies."
3. In *Get Together Americans,* Rachel describes a session in a city-wide black-out. During the event, Josh White sings "Summertime" from the show Porgy and Bess, which opened on stage in 1935 (See Wiki, accessed 19 May 2019). The year should have been between 1936 and 1937 for this black-out.
4. Narrator for Program # 10, the Germans.
5. Narrator at end of Program #10, the Germans.
6. These supporters included Hollingsworth Wood, Eduard C. Johnson, and Rabbi Milton Steinberg.

References

Bianchi, William. 2008. *Schools of the Air: A History of Instructional Programs on Radio in the United States.* Jefferson, NC: McFarland and Company.

Cremin, Lawrence. 1961. *The Transformation of the School.* New York: Vintage.

———. 1977. *Traditions in American Education.* New York: Basic Books.

Crispin, George A. 1987. *Rachel Davis DuBois: Founded of the Group Conversation as an Adult Educational Facilitator for Reducing Intercultural Strife.* Unpublished EdD diss., Temple University.

deLima, Agnes. 1926. *Our Enemy the Child.* New York: New Republic.

DuBois, Rachel. 1930. "Measuring Attitudes." *Friends Intelligencer,* June, pp. 467–468.

———. 1932. "Shall We Emotionalize Our Students?" *Friends Intelligencer,* December, pp. 973–974.

———. 1935. Our Enemy the Stereotype. *Progressive Education,* 145–150.

---. 1936. *Danger or Promise?* Speech at San Francisco State College.

---. 1939. "The Need for Sharing Cultural Values." *Friends Intelligence*, February, pp. 84–85.

---. 1943. *Get Together Americans: Friendly Approaches to Racial and Cultural Conflicts Through the Neighborhood-Home Festival.* New York: Harper & Brothers.

---. 1946. "The Face-to-Face Group as a Unit for a Program of Intercultural Education." *Journal of Educational Sociology* 19 (9): 555–561.

---. 1984. *(ATSM) All This and Something More: Pioneering in Intercultural Education.* Bryn Mawr: Dorrance.

Durkheim, Emile. 1956. *Education and Sociology.* Trans. and with an Introd. Sherwood D. Fox, Foreword by Talcott Parsons. New York: The Free Press.

Graham, Patricia Albjerg. 1967. *Progressive Education: From Arcady to Academe.* New York: Teachers College Press.

Hamm, Thomas D. 2003. *The Quakers in America.* New York: Columbia University Press.

Jewish Publication Society. 1955. *The Holy Scriptures.* Philadelphia: The Jewish Publication Society of America.

Kaplan, Mordechai. 1934. *Judaism as a Civilization: Toward a Reconstruction of Jewish Life.* New York: Macmillan.

Kulp, Daniel H., II. 1932. *Educational Sociology.* New York: Longmans.

Lemann, Nicholas. 2000. *The Big Test.* New York: Farrar, Straus, and Giroux.

Mitchell, Lucy Sprague. 1953. *Two Lives: The Story of Wesley Clair Mitchell and Myself.* New York: Simon and Schuster.

Montalto, Nicholas V. 1977. *The Forgotten Dream: A History of the Intercultural Education Movement 1924–1941.* Unpublished PhD diss., University of Minnesota.

Newman, Joseph W. 2002. "Marietta Johnson and the Organic School". In *Founding Mothers and Others: Women Educational Leaders During the Progressive Era*, ed. Alan R. Sadovnik, and Susan Semel, 19–36. New York: Palgrave.

Pratt, Caroline. 1917. "The Play School." In *Bulletin #3.* New York: Bureau of Educational Experiments.

---. 1948/1970. *I Learn from Children.* New York: Perennial Harper & Row.

Roosevelt, Franklin. 1939. Statement on "Americans All-Immigrants All". Washington, DC: Government Printing Office.

Smith, Walter Robinson. 1917/2017. *An Introduction to Educational Sociology.* Reprint. Delhi: Facsimile Publisher.

Thomas, W.I. 1921/1971. *Old World Traits Transplanted.* Montclair, NJ: Patterson – Smith Publishers.

CHAPTER 7

The Great Segue of 1941 and the Refreshment of Rachel's Concern

A segue is an uninterrupted transition from one key to another with no break in tune. In music, a segue might be a transition from one key to another while keeping the song. For Rachel her segue came in the form of her break from the Service Bureau into self-discovery that allowed her to carry on in her Concern trying not to miss a beat, focusing on the main tenets of her work to explore the within of herself so she could continue reaching out to serve a greater good, "Dreaming Ahead," and continuing to place those dreams into practice.

This account represents a bridge across an intense time, one month, August of 1941, when Rachel was pained and exhausted from her ordeal with the Service Bureau. She literally stumbled upon a program that would potentially give her tools to refresh her spiritual and intellectual nourishment beyond what Quaker meeting could provide. It was fellow Friend Harold Chance who suggested Rachel might gain insight and relief from a month-long workshop led by philosopher Gerald Heard (1889–1971) on spirituality and culture. Perhaps they could guide her to psychic and intellectual health through his wisdom. At the outset, it seemed like the experience would help in relation to Rachel's work. What happened, however, was the workshop brought her to understand that her past *before* she embarked on her career, had much to do with her current situation and her future.

This was an interesting turn of events. A Quaker, when he or she had a problem to resolve, he or she usually turned to the Meeting for counsel.

One turned inward, not outward. But Rachel's dilemma was something not initially related to Quaker faith and practice. Rachel needed a special counsel for healing which the Meeting could not provide (personal communication, Haring 18 May 2019). In attending a Heard workshop, Rachel was taking a risk, jumping into a great unknown.

Henry Fitzgerald Heard possessed a wide range of interests and knowledge. The son of an Anglo-Irish clergyman, Heard was born in London and was expected to follow in his father's footsteps. But Gerald's insatiable curiosity led him not to follow his father. He earned the honors in history from Oxford College in 1911 and took a master's degree to explore parapsychology, Vedanta belief, and the philosophy of religions. He hosted a radio series on science on the British Broadcasting Corporation (BBC) and authored some 35 books on his thought as well some mysteries under the pen name of H. F. Heard. In 1937 he and his friend Aldous Huxley came to the United States, first for Heard to chair the Historical Anthropology program at Duke University. After one semester, Heard decided to apply his thinking elsewhere. He (and Huxley) relocated to southern California to continue research and create an Esalen-like[1] environment for spiritual and cultural enlightenment through the development of human potential first at LaVerne College and then at Trabuco monastery (www.geraldheard.com).

Prior to the establishment of the workshops at LaVerne and Trabuco, Heard was involved with Pendle Hill stalwarts, the Brintons, in 1938. They had a shared interest in psychology, science, and religion, and in 1943, Pendle Hill supporters formed the Friends Conference on Religion and Psychology. As of 2011, this conference was continuing its explorations into the intersection of mind and faith (https://pendlehill.org).

Heard worked with the Society of Friends as well as with the Pacific Coast Institute of International Affairs. His center on his wisdom and the encouragement for others to rise on the wind of evolution was an exciting topic for Rachel, as she was interested in science and mysticism, something she had on her mind since the landing of the turkey buzzard on her chest when she was a child. It also meshed with the mysteries and realities of *Dreaming Ahead*. And so, she enrolled in a Heard workshop held at LaVerne College outside of Los Angeles.

Her description of Heard, the person, was at once spiritual and comical: "He looked like some of the paintings of Jesus. He had a rather small head starting with a large forehead, and ending with a pointed beard. What a brain!" (*ATSM*, 100).

According to Rachel, it was Heard's philosophy that the universe is one organic evolving whole, held together by the power of Love, and that each of us is an integral part of it. On the one hand, this reminded Rachel of the behaviorism espoused by J. B. Watson who believed education was a matter of conditioning. She did not agree with this. Rather, she found the evolutional teaching of John Dewey more fitting, which he explained in his book *Human Nature and Conduct* (1930): "The act must come before the thought; the thought must come before the habit; and the habit must come before the ability to produce the thought at will" (Dewey 1930, 30–31). Education, as Dewey looked at it, and as her professors discussed it, was this cumulative, ongoing process, a collection of experiences and an application of them to learn about the worlds around us. Evolution is ongoing and it had reached a stage where humans had to be a deliberate participant. Unlike her professors at Teachers College and NYU, Heard looked at development combining intellectual and spiritual terms, relating it to Jesus in John 15:15: "Henceforth I call you not servants; for the servant knoweth not what his lord doeth: but I have called you friends." Heard's interpretations of life was that "up to the point of the arrival of humanity, the direction of evolution was determined by an external cosmic force. From now on we must cooperate with that cosmic power we call God or the Power of Love" (*ATSM*, 101). This is the task of religion, psychology, and science today—the science of consciousness.

Take away the evangelical bent to Heard, and one can relate to some of the basic tenets of Educational Sociology. The school is a living and breathing organism. Educational Sociology's task is to discern the parts and pieces human and otherwise that keep the school alive. While parts and pieces make up the physical plant, they also refer to the conduct of education as a human interactive endeavor. Education is evolution, and for Dewey and for Heard, such an enterprise must be consciously performed through the development of habits leading to awareness of acts.

Why did Rachel choose to go to the workshop in California when she could have gone to Pendle Hill, a Quaker retreat and study center outside of Philadelphia? The reasons why lie in their focus and offerings. Pendle Hill, founded in 1930, was named for the hill in Lancashire, England, where George Fox received his calling to found Quakerism. In its history, Pendle Hill is described as "a Quaker study center designed to prepare its adult students for service in the Religious Society of Friends and in the world." Its mission was (and still is) educational and religious, rooted in Quaker community life, faith, and practice, in addition to intellectual pursuits, including the provision of bedroom/studies for those wishing a quiet place to write (https://pendlehill.org).

Heard's workshop was initially based at LaVerne College outside of Los Angeles. In 1942, the workshop physically transferred to a nearby facility, and named "Trabuco" which translated to English from Spanish means (1) a blunderbuss—the short-range shotgun; and (2) an insensitive blundering person (*Free Dictionary*). There is no stated reason how Trabuco got its name. Heard's historical and intellectual estate is held by a literary executor, and Heard is held for admiration and erudition through a website, www.geraldheard.com, consisting of biographical sketches of Heard, testimonies, a bibliography of Heard's writings, and a section for those wishing to make donations to keep the website and materials available to the public. Unfortunately, pages of manuscripts in the site are not paginated, and one must tap on links embedded in the whole. For all intents and purposes, the workshop at LaVerne and Trabuco are interchangeable in description. The only difference lies in Trabuco being a long-term residence venture in a different location.

Timothy Miller, in his biographical sketch on Heard and Trabuco, quotes Heard: "Trabuco begins its work in a spirit of humble and open-minded enquiry. There are no "prophets" among us. We all start from the beginning, bringing nothing but our need for God and our trust in His Grace without which search for Him is in vain. Trabuco hopes to grow, spiritually and organically, as the growth of its members progresses. Our ultimate structure may be a modern version of the medieval university" (Miller n.d. www.geraldheard.com).

LaVerne and Trabuco were experiments in the development of human potential. As opposed to the Protestant thought of the Quakers, Trabuco was founded on Heard's new-found commitment to the Vedanta tradition, the search for self-knowledge as well as the search for God (Vedanta Society of Southern California, 2016; personal communication, David, 25 May 2019). It caused him to question the particles of other faiths, their tenets, and practices, including the question of what lay in the mind of the Quaker who goes into the silence of meeting for worship, but this in particular was something he chose not to challenge with Rachel; at least she chose not to write about it.

Pendle Hill and Trabuco shared some practices, but they were different in style. The participants at Pendle Hill engaged in silent worship morning and evening. Those engaged with Heard meditated three times a day (morning, noon, and night). People shared in meals at both retreats, and they also assisted in upkeep of the site. The difference for Rachel was that at Pendle Hill she would be in the sheltering arms of her faith. With Heard, she would be out of her comfort zone and constantly prodded into thought *and feeling*. She needed to be challenged, not comforted. That is why she took the risk. She knew herself well enough in terms of her learning process. Confrontation through experience was paramount.

Rachel did not write about Heard's involvement with the Quakers. When she arrived for the Heard workshop, she became immediately immersed in the workshop and its activities. It was in the workshop that she started making connections between science and faith, connections she first felt as a child. As a child she didn't know what to think about her experience, wondering if it was a kind of message from the Divine. It made her feel awkward and out of step. Heard helped her make the connection as he spoke to the concept of "consciousness." He explained "that evolution is an ongoing process that had reached a stage where humanity had to be a deliberate participant" (*ATSM*, 101). This participation required a recasting of relationships that demanded new faculties of the mind, one of which "empathy as deeper than sympathy" (*ATSM*, 101). The faculty Heard was referring to was the capacity for understanding other people's feelings. Rachel felt she was lacking in this capacity, and she added it to her list of interpersonal qualities that she wanted to improve on.

The other quality of importance to Rachel was that of being contemplative. She felt she was lacking in that skill as well. She decided "that regular meditation could provide me the center, the power, and the spiritual energy to carry on my active work" (*ATSM*, 101). She needed the powers of both forethought and hindsight that could be applied in everyday life.

Rachel was not one for exuberant "Ah ha!" moments. Instead she made quiet connections, applications of information, thought, and practice that she could file and call upon for use when needed. In fact, this was what the Heard workshop was about—making connections to further human potential based on gleanings from science, religion, and psychology—the culmination of culture.

A day in the life of a Heard workshop consisted of meditation, communal mealtimes where participants ate in silence while another participant read aloud from the works of various mystics. Between 9 p.m. and 9 a.m., participants observed what Rachel called "Benedictine Silence." (*ATSM*, 101) During the day, participants learned of the other thoughts of mystics in classroom-like settings and in informal discussions about Heard's interactions of mind and culture, science, and religion.

A highlight of the workshop was the one-on-one visit with Heard. When Rachel met with him, she was emotionally raw and was ready to vent. He listened and offered this: "Once we can understand our past, we can realize that we have a future. In brief that future is to evolve further, to evolve continuously, to evolve consciousness. We have to look forward to, to aim and achieve a further condition of consciousness. As cunning turned into foresight, so foresight in turn becomes reflection; as reflection grows into speculation, so speculation grows into self-consciousness, this detached awareness of oneself, must be followed by another step that looms ahead of us" (Heard 1971, 13). Heard gave Rachel a sense of direction: to understand where you are, you need to know where you have been. To know where you are and where you have been, you prepare for the future. This is accomplished through the construction of the evergrowing, always revolving, never-ending consciousness.

But how to get to this place? What Heard was saying made sense, but what did getting to this "place" look like? Heard provided the metaphor of a ladder consisting of three rungs: (1) Purgation; (2) Liberation and Enlightenment; and (3) Union, or completion, each corresponding to three beings: the novice, the proficient, and the perfect (Heard 1971, 15–18). Purgation is the most difficult of rungs to step on and stay on to maintain its challenges. What this rung boiled down to was the reduction of ego, stripping the self of hindrances to proficiency and perfection. Purgation? Losing ego? This must have taken Rachel by surprise. After all, the last ten years were full of affronts to her ego, already leaving her feeling bare. Her goal for attending the workshop was to regain a sense of self, replenish her soul, and not deplete herself of what energies she had in reserve. But that was not what Heard intended. He saw purgation as never-ending, part of a long, involved, though painful process. To start the journey, he gave Rachel a mantra: "I am nothing. Thou art all": "I tried it, over and over, hour by hour, until once being in an almost sleep-like trance, I suddenly became fully conscious and I realized I was saying "'Thou art nothing. I am All.'" She now had her one powerful "Ah ha! Moment." She understood that losing the ego was not losing the self. It was a gaining of self, liberated, enlightened, and united on a manageable path (*ATSM*, 102). Now she would have to walk and talk a new way of being, alert and willing to take on the first rung.

Besides the pain of the last ten years, what else did Rachel need to purge? She needed to shed the persistent doubt she had regarding her pacifism that came from the time when she purchased a War Bond. She needed to discard the remnants of the awkwardness she felt as a child. Her experience at Bucknell was another sore point. Although she wrote she didn't want to be a part of the school's social life, maybe the ache she felt was more persistent than she cared to admit. As for her trial by fire with the Woodbury Board of Education and the American Legion, she was challenged and hurt by the experience. After all, she was a life resident of the town and her family was well known through its activities in Meeting and at the Grange. It was like an onion of painful layers of self to peel away and consider.

Others in the workshop had their own intense experiences with Heard during those private meetings. They and she bonded, becoming a "sharing-caring" group (*ATSM*, 102). When they weren't meditating, sharing meals, and attending classes, this 22-member group had time to talk about their lives outside of the workshop. For Rachel this meant talking about the Assembly, the Group Conversation Method, and the Neighborhood-Home Festival.

It was through the "sharing-caring" and Heard's "ladder" that Rachel realized that what she was doing, workwise especially in the planning phases of the Assembly, Group Conversation, and the Neighborhood-Home Festival. To get to the place where the goals of programs involved expressing misconceptions and biases in order to produce events with their own goals of consciousness raising, planners had to engage purgation. To reduce the ego, program planners worked at admitting their cultural biases and learning about the realities of immigrant life and its contributions to the United States. Through purgation, they were to become free of stereotypes and misgivings, which would lead to enlightenment and union, an ultimate consciousness. The hope was that such a journey up the ladder would extend to everyone involved in the programs in which each rung of the ladder had "sub-rungs" reflecting the personal and the professional. To think in terms of an alignment, in the three basic building blocks, the emotional, situational, and intellectual, purgation was essential. It would consist of purgation in planning and then in exposing participants to cultural difference. The rung of enlightenment and liberation aligns with the intellectual component, the study of culture groups when information on their contributions would enlighten, would shed light on the subject, and further liberate one from stereotype and misconceptions. The highest rung union is a rung of encouragement of social commerce, that opportunity to be informal, to visit with program representatives.

Being in each being—novice, the proficient, and the perfect—is never-ending. With each new situation, one at once climbs the rungs and achieves the states of being. The states are more fleeting, whereas the climb up the rungs is a constant activity with outcomes that can be experienced, and as one worked on the ladder, expected. And for Rachel, this was the process of what one could call "conscious tolerance." To have a successful program to encourage tolerance, being personally aware of the process is vital in approaching the outcome.

Rachel's experience in the Heard workshop was intensely personal. It did, however, pull together her approach to Intercultural Education and settle it into her heart. Of the three elements, she encountered the emotional, the intellectual, and the social in her meditations, discussions with other workshop attendees, and her session with Heard. The workshop experience added a new dimension to Rachel's understanding of the five wishes introduced in graduate school. Her wishes, when she entered the workshop, were more like "longings." She longed to be recognized for her contributions to Intercultural Education; she found a place where she longed to respond to her spirituality without judgment. The workshop met a longing for new experience, a chance experience longed for, for communication and reflection, and it provided a longed-for safe place for doing so. Last, as an opportunity for experience beyond the self, Heard's advice to reduce the ego challenged Rachel to do something she needed and sometimes longed to do, to walk in different shoes, to look at life from another's point of view. This was her time to reflect, respond, and be reflexive. And in the quest for enlightenment and union, Rachel would ultimately create a pair of new-fitting shoes of her own, a metaphor for the walk to consciousness.

The Heard workshop was not a quick fix for Rachel, but it did arm her with a refreshed resolve for activism and a new strengthening of her Concern. At the end of the month, she returned to New York, and with others from the workshop, they met for further discussion of Heard's principles. The doors of the Service Bureau may have been closed, but thanks, in part to the Heard workshop, a new door, one of continued group conversation and intensified school programming, opened wide and Rachel gamely entered as a provider and as a seeker of conscious tolerance and everlasting consciousness.

Note

1. Esalen Institute was founded in 1962 by Stanford University classmates Michael Murphy and Dick Price. Its design was inspired, in part by conversations with Heard, Murphy, and Price. The Institute offers opportunities for self-discovery through spiritual and psychological means.

References

Dewey, John. 1930. *Human Nature and Conduct: An Introduction to Social Psychology*. New York: The Modern Library.

DuBois, Rachel Davis. 1984. *(ATSM) All This and Something More: Pioneering in Intercultural Education*. Bryn Mawr: Dorrance.

Heard, Gerald. 1971. *Training for the Life of the Spirit*. Eugene, OR: Wipf and Stock Publishers.

Miller, Timothy. n.d. Gerald Heard. www.geraldheard.com.

CHAPTER 8

Closing Doors, Opening Anew: The Workshop for Cultural Democracy, the *Parranda*, and Facing Joseph McCarthy (1941–1953)

When Rachel came to Heard's workshop, she was emotionally drained, intellectually challenged, and socially adrift. Her experience with the Heard seminar gave her the opportunity for "20–20 hindsight" which let her see her situation and refresh her resolve to continue on the path of her Concern. Returning to New York, she was stronger and continued to serve the public with Intercultural Education courses using Group Conversation and the Neighborhood-Home Festival as ways of emotionalizing participants, fostering intercultural growth through a combination of educational practice, increasing knowledge about cultures—attention to the school and community as a living organism, and above all, enlarging capacities for tolerance (Deafenbaugh 2017).

If it wasn't for the Heard workshop, Rachel would not have had the emotional stamina to continue her work. Heard's imagery of the ladder and its three rungs: Purgation, Enlightenment, and Union were signposts to consciousness, which Rachel needed to go through herself, realizing too that this is what she wanted in people who were investing their energies in learning about and planning programs and procedures to learn of the immigrant experience: they needed to reduce ego first and foremost by shedding misconceptions about the people in their midst before they could create a program designed to meet and quash those very same misconceptions and biases in others. She wanted sharing-caring relationships between

© The Author(s) 2019
J. Rosenberg, *Intercultural Education, Folklore, and the Pedagogical Thought of Rachel Davis DuBois*,
https://doi.org/10.1007/978-3-030-26222-8_8

everyone involved in her work, and she felt that such relations would bring "joy" and "love" to all.[1]

In matters of the heart, she had her relationship with Nathan to reckon with. By this time, theirs was no longer a "50–50" marriage with Rachel spending all of her time in New York City with her work and Nathan in New Jersey with his work. He and the housekeeper, he and Rachel had hired when Rachel started spending more time in New York City, were beginning to take a romantic turn toward one another. To this end, Rachel and Nathan divorced on 1 January 1942. Recall that early in their engagement, Nathan informed Rachel that he could not father children (Chap. 4), so they didn't have any. No alimony was involved (*ATSM*, 105).

There were other New Yorkers at the Seminar, and they and Rachel met to share a light pot-luck supper and listen and discuss aspects of Heard's writings. This was a part of Rachel's personal "reconstruction program," where, in addition to her understandings of Heard, she intensified her strength in "Dreaming Ahead," which solidified her Concern to an even greater degree (*ATSM*, 105). As the group dwindled, the Workshop for Cultural Democracy seemed to naturally slide into place. It functioned as the Intercultural Education Workshop from 1941 to 1946. In 1946 it received recognition from the Internal Revenue Service (IRS) as a 501 (c)(3) as the Workshop for Cultural Democracy, the Board of which was made up of Rachel's supporters from the Service Bureau, teachers, community members, education sociologists, and others, including folklorist Ben Botkin who shared Rachel's Concern and her way of approaching it through the heritage and traditions of the people. In its application to the IRS, the stated objective of the Workshop was "to develop means for positive approaches to race and culture conflicts and offer teacher training to its approaches."[2]

The Workshop was more activist-centered compared to the Service Bureau for Intercultural Education. In an undated promotional pamphlet, the Workshop was defined, "as the name states, first of all a workshop—a social laboratory which works out and tests ways of eradicating prejudice and building friendship." "[I]t believes in cultural democracy—the freedom for Americans of every race, creed, social status, and national origin to pursue happiness in their own ways; and the building of a rich American culture out of the best in these diverse cultural strains."[3] The Workshop provided the public with at least five services: (1) continuing the Neighborhood-Home Festival; (2) developing and providing resource materials highlighting culture group contributions to American society;

(3) advocating and consulting directly with issues brought to them from the outside, especially those dealing with race and culture; (4) training teachers in the execution of assemblies; and (5) making available Rachel's publications on the Assembly and the Neighborhood-Home Festival. Rachel continued executing her programs using the three elements first outlined in Chap. 5—the emotion, intellect, and social presence, along with the five wishes for recognition, response, experience, safety, and an experience outside of the comfort zone offered when she was studying under Kulp, and what I call the "four I-s" for programming: (1) inform; (2) involve; (3) invite; and (4) influence. The overall structure behind all of these actions is a cultural drama that embraces concerns and the people who have them. These actions were tested throughout Rachel's graduate school training and her work with the Service Bureau for Intercultural Education, and the results were consistently positive—they were best practices—which will be explored in the Conclusions.

The programs Rachel designed explicitly applied folklore, including talk about holidays, songs, courting customs, crafts, foods, and games to stimulate talk and forge a sense of peace in a time where peace was threatened by turns of events in politics, economics, and, most importantly, war. Her thought had the support of the President, Franklin Roosevelt: "We are rich in the elements from which to weave a culture. In blending these elements into a national fabric of unity and strength let us keep the original fibers so intact that the fineness of each will show in the completed handiwork."[4]

Rachel engaged her pen. Her articles were timely attempts to bring intercultural education to cultural democracy, which would lead to social justice which in turn would lead to democracy—it was essential for defense and peace. She wrote,

> the total defense of our democracy, it seems to me, means we must pay special attention to intercultural education until its objectives become firmly woven into general education. This means [the] definite provision in curricular and extra-curricular activities in schools throughout the country from kindergarten through college for a recognition of the part each group has played in the building of our country … sharing with each other the best of our traditions, customs, and folkways. … we must attempt to produce a feeling of pride not only in what the individual is, but also in what his culture group is. … the best way to overcome a feeling of inferiority is to develop a feeling that we are parts of all humanity and its accomplishments. (1941a, 69)

In the tangle of national politics, Rachel explained "What is Needed for Democracy's Defense" focusing on the humanity in being a part of the world: "Democracy's defense ... depends partly and perhaps basically on a better distribution of the good things of life, and partly on equal civil and political rights. But in the realm of the intangible it depends on holding on to that which is valuable in our unique social backgrounds, and on sharing it with others so that a richer American culture may be developed. If America has a destiny, it is that we have a chance to work out a microcosm of world unity. If any of us are left to pick up the pieces after this war, there must be more, not less democracy, and the world culture which will evolve must be based on a sharing of cultural values on a world basis. The East and West will meet in a creative use of differences. ... In a democracy of sharing there is no domination. When we have attained that level, we can begin to build a world culture, for humanity is one organic whole, and life means not only to give but to be willing to receive from that whole" (1941b, 70). Given the focus of the Workshop on culture as a dynamic and an evolving state of being, its work would not have survived if that dynamic of diversity was not recognized nationally (or even internationally). Achieving that recognition of the elements of our worlds that make us who we are, Rachel warned of one thing: *ethnocentrism* "and realize that we are all God's children. I feel that this development can come about only if, besides knowing what we have in our backgrounds to be proud of, we also know our shortcomings. Then and then only will we want to share, for sharing means taking as well as giving. Only thus we can use our human and spiritual resources. Only thus can we build a richer American culture" (1941a, 70). Ethnocentrism was the one thing that could destroy the Workshop whose mission ultimately rested on equality for all races, religions, socio-economic status, and political alliance. The Workshop did not welcome Father Coughlin's call for a Christian, White America. Instead, it stayed strong in the belief that ours was our nation. Rachel ultimately wrote, "Mankind needs to find ways to generate enough spiritual cohesion to enable human beings to cooperate" (1945).

With World War II, the nation pulled together to produce and use what was needed for the war effort, from cans to tires. Posters plastered walls: "Loose lips sink ships," and other reminders that while the United States is great, it is still vulnerable, as the attack on Pearl Harbor showed. The Workshop continued with the above-listed services. Intercultural Education was now cast for its "grassroots" nature. Ethel Duncan, writing on *Democracy's Children* wrote, "Intercultural Education is a grass-roots movement. The classroom teacher and classroom pupils represent the starting point, insofar as the schools are concerned in this movement. A class is potentially, or in reality, a unified group capable of being led into acting together in a constructive way. ... It is ... a making use of the opportunities which arise ... for the development of attitude of appreciation and understanding" (1945, 2). The school on the large scale and the classroom on the small were examples of sharing-caring communities that could support appreciation and understanding.

In 1945, the Workshop was called into action by JPS (Junior High School) 165, the Robert Simons School. The program that was devised for the school was a perfect application of Workshop aims, principles, and practices through an understanding of the school considering its internal and community folklore and culture and how to preserve tradition while effecting social change, a "capacity for tolerance." Rachel developed a guide for this school's issue, published in 1950 as *Neighbors in Action: A Manual for Local Leaders in Intergroup Relations (NIA)*.

The problem at JPS 165 was one of volume and content. By 1945 40% of the school population was Puerto Rican and consisted of some 48 different culture groups (*NIA*, 15). The school's parent's organization realized that the Puerto Rican students were not included in Parents Association sponsored activities, due in part by a language barrier. The Parents Association wanted to fix the situation. A fourth-grade teacher, Mrs. Fischer, learned about the Workshop through a presentation of its work to The Council on Community Action, and she suggested to JPS 165 Principal Dr. George Kurke that the Workshop might aid in bringing relief, respect, and release for cultural diversity which would lead to the creation of a cultural democracy in the school. Rachel met with the principal and the Parents Association and decided that the Workshop could help. In doing so, she made the following stipulations which reflected the mission of the Workshop:

1. To experiment further with group conversation as one method of providing face-to-face experiences which will motivate "grassroots" citizens to work together as neighbors on their common problem of living together.
2. To provide similar intercultural experiences for parents and children so that the home and school may pull together toward common goals.
3. To aid in overcoming various kinds of intergroup prejudices and tensions in an indirect and positive way to the end that people in a

given community may more easily work together to solve their common problems of living together.
4. To move forward in the implementation of the goals involved in the concept of cultural democracy.
5. To find more effective ways to train local leaders "on the job" so that they can assume a more intelligent role in overcoming prejudices and in developing understanding attitudes among themselves and their neighbors (*NIA*, 1950, 24–26).

These stipulations embraced everything the Workshop stood for, and the next steps came forth. Intense Group Conversation method over a period of eight sessions was used to sensitize and inform the Parents Association, the teachers, all students' families, and the Puerto Rican community about their differences and commonalities. The Workshop would invite all in exploring possible avenues to take in alleviating tensions. The Parents Association, consisting of parents, teachers, and students, would be involved in the design and execution of whatever program or project that was born from their deliberations. What came out of the program/project developments and actions would, in turn, hopefully influence and encourage a shift in attitudes, from the negative to the positive for all parties.

The process from informing to influencing was very structured, another drama in three acts that Rachel applied to the Assembly and the Neighborhood-Home Festival. To explore topics for programming, the first act was a time for planning: exploring self with others. Here Rachel met with parents and teachers, using Group Conversation to explore attitudes and outline and forward project possibilities, from breadth to depth. In the beginning, the Puerto Rican mothers in attendance expressed the feeling that they were being pushed out of the way when it came to their sons and daughters (*ATSM*, 124). In Group Conversations designed to develop leadership among the adults, the mothers in the Parents Association and Puerto Rican community shared some of their traditions, including lace making and cooking. In the course of conversation, one of the Puerto Rican mothers, Mrs. Torres, described a kind of Puerto Rican party, the *Parranda*, where people would spend an evening going from home to home for visiting, and she suggested that the party could be translated into a school activity where students would visit the homes of select culture bearers, learn about key traditions, and participants would be fortified with a sampling of traditional foods or some other form of expressive culture. The group decided that the *Parranda* would be a way of bringing students, the school community, and the community surrounding the school together. As a culmination of elements and wishes, it was the school's element of surprise for itself and others (*NIA*, 38–39). It was the second act of the play. When the fieldtrip ended, participants review the experience in light of what they experienced—the third act.

The *Parranda* fit within the three elements and five wishes of Educational Sociology. Between 1946 and 1950, 55 *Parrandas* took place (Harlam 1950, 2), and parents, community members, and the general public were involved as visitors, and the public was invited to hear about this program and how it fostered intercultural harmony. Reporting on the party, it was recognized as one of the most intensive of projects. Three groups were fully and equally involved: (1) the family; (2) the school; and (3) the community.

Blanche Schwartz, a JPS teacher, wrote of seven functions of the *Parranda* (1948):

1. Develops self-confidence and poise: the ability to form, express, and defend one's own opinions and to work with others.
2. Fosters civic attitudes and understanding of socio-economic questions within the child's experience and comprehension.
3. Develop the habit of critical consideration of problems, people, and events and clear thinking of them.
4. Trains pupils in a democratic way of living.
5. Cultivates sympathetic and helpful relationships between parents and teachers, and utilizes the home and the community as significant educational resources.
6. Fosters the understanding and practice of desirable social relationships.
7. Engenders appreciation and desire for worthwhile practices (1948, 16).

Adult and student reaction to the *Parranda* was very positive. Comments were invited, and both the Workshop and JPS 165 shared awareness and desired solutions via the party:
Students:

1. "All schools should have *Parrandas*. We learn more on them than in school. A lot of people in New York City are lonesome. They want us to make friends, and the *Parrandas* help people to get along with other people."

2. "They get people together, so they feel like relatives."
3. "People feel they belong to one another and all together."

Adults:

1. "We get to know people in our own neighborhood."
2. "This will make the children more friendly and stop their fighting so much" (*NIA*, 1950, 208).

Students, parents, and teachers were mostly positive, their negative attitudes shifted into a positive range. The *Parranda* was the idea of the culture group, the Puerto Ricans, who were originally met with fear, a fear of the unknown. Through Group Conversations and the *Parrandas* themselves, tensions between the Puerto Rican students and their families eased because everyone worked hard to shed their biases in order to encourage students and others to do the same. There were those associated with JPS 165, however, who could not release their antipathy. There were continued racist attitudes toward the African American. Another doubter could not comprehend how the *Parranda* would ease anti-Semitic disease (*NIA*, 211–212). What these naysayers did not realize was the *Parranda* consisted of many methods aimed at the *encouragement of awareness* and the use of culture(s) in promoting democracy through education. Awareness is essential to cultural democracy which acts like a bowl cradling the essentials of cultural being which starts at home and in the classroom. This will be addressed in the Conclusions.

Rachel was able to show the "me" of culture group and the shift toward what she called "neighborliness" in democracy, or the "we": "If our democracy is to function ... our cultural diversity needs to be as normal in American life as are different makes of automobiles, and the various customs of our neighbors as natural as different types of airplanes" (*NIA*, 230). She knew it would be difficult but she believed it was possible: "It is the depth and quality of our feeling about other people which count when it comes to being willing to struggle together to bring about social reform or even to eliminate prejudice" (*NIA*, 233).

The first *Parranda* took place during Spring Break in the evening. It was successful enough that the new principal Dr. Henry Antell suggested that the event take place for seventh graders during the school day. They were using a new social studies curriculum for seventh grade, and the *Parranda* was deemed a powerful lesson, learning in situ. It led Rachel to write, "If school and community organizations would plan many ways of giving social recognition to each cultural group in American life and especially those in immediate communities [,] a spirit of give and take would soon be released that would make easier the development of neighborliness which is basic to cultural interaction" (*NIA*, 233).

TALE FROM THE FIELD: A SCHOOL FIELDTRIP

A school fieldtrip is close to the *Parranda* in terms of intent, logistics, content, and execution. Unlike the *Parranda*, community members do not participate in Group Conversation to discuss academic and social need. Rather, this is something we learn from interactions with teachers, principals, students, tradition bearers, and community members in individualized, usually one-time meetings. Given the nature of a Folk Arts in Education (FAIE) program which I described in Chap. 4, the fieldtrip is born from the structure of the daily program. The difference with the FAIE program, as it takes place in the classroom and the fieldtrip, is that the fieldtrip heightens cultural connections *on the home turf of the tradition bearer*. In a sense, the students become Other amid the tradition bearer's life rather than the other way around when the tradition bearer comes to the school.

Logistically, a fieldtrip has certain components prior to actual execution that are like the *Parranda*. For the fieldtrip to happen, the principal approves the plan so that the teacher and class can do the fieldtrip, so they are allowed to go off campus for a day. In terms of planning, the school system coordinates transportation—a bus and driver to take student and teacher to the fieldtrip site. When time comes to go on the fieldtrip, the class (including the teacher and interested adults) is prepared for the adventure by learning about the featured tradition bearer and identifying questions that the visitors could ask the tradition bearer about his or her life and work.

Once at the site, students and teachers on the bus were sometimes greeted by the tradition bearers who came on to the bus to talk about their lives and what students might experience on this trip. The bus was a moving classroom that would contain excitement and focus on information that the students might have had contact with to prepare for an informed invitation to explore a craft and lifestyle that would highlight the life of the tradition bearers as "ordinary people doing extraordinary things." This is different from the *Parranda* because the visitors in a *Parranda* are greeted when they arrive at the host's door, but the hosts, too, are ordinary people doing extraordinary things through their cultures.

With the fieldtrips I've put together, there were considerations of size. Whereas in a setting where I presented to separate classes of 25 more or less, I co-joined students, so the usually separated classes are put together as one. With the fieldtrip, the two classes are joined, increasing class size. This requires participation of the teachers to cover 50 fourth graders.

On one trip, students and teachers went to the work shed and home of a Mr. and Mrs. R. Mr. R. was known for his creation of furniture from cypress procured from regional sources, which he learned from his father. He not only made furniture from cypress, his and his wife's house was also constructed from cypress, including walls, chairs at a dining table, and a bedroom suite. Mr. and Mrs. R. worked with me to coordinate the visit. First Mr. and Mrs. R. came on the bus to be introduced and share a bit about their lives, focusing on how they were from the area and that Mr. R. learned furniture making from his father. We decided that while one class would visit with Mr. R. in the shop and explore and see how he made the furniture; the other class would go to the house where Mrs. R. shared how and where the cypress was used downstairs with the dining area and bedroom suite. At the workshop, students gathered in a semi-circle; the furniture maker showed his tools, demonstrated how to strip the bark from the cypress using a machete, and how he shaped the cypress to create, for demonstration purposes, an armchair. He invited students to try their hand at stripping bark, standing behind them, guiding their arms as they wielded the machete.

When the class ended their visit to the workshop, they walked up the drive to the house with a teacher while another teacher would take students from the house to the workshop. This arrangement worked well, and thankfully, the weather was good for the workshop and leading to the house.

Back in the classroom, we discussed our experience and shared opinions. The students expressed wonder over the fact that this couple led such a life bound by tradition, and they thought cypress furniture was "cool." This was, in Rachel's terms, an emotional exposure to the craftsman, his wife, and their chosen lifestyle. Intellectually, the prior knowledge about cypress furniture making in their state gave them the opportunity to connect past with present in a visceral way, and in subject areas, for example, students could study the flora of the area where the cypress was procured, math in light of selecting sizes of branches for furniture, language arts in writings thank-you notes to those visited. As for the social component, being able to talk with the tradition bearers on the bus, and informally, led to a greater appreciation of the tradition and the lifestyle and the fact that these people were no better or worse than they were.

Fieldtrips, like the *Parranda*, are positive communication adventures. They take the student out of the protective space of the classroom, and through careful planning with teachers and hosts, students are assured of a safe place for learning through experience. Thankfully, our work in folklife education has structures for protection. Because we are basically attached to a school, we are supported with little question. Unfortunately, for Rachel, that did not happen, and in June 1953, her world, once more, was turned on its ear.

The Workshop for Cultural Democracy was doing well. Rachel was teaching courses on Intercultural Education, and she was called on occasion to consult schools and organizations on their intercultural efforts. On a Friday night in the first week of June, Rachel had returned from New York after working in Chicago for two months with Ukrainian immigrants and their integration into Chicago's life. She had invited a friend, Peg Thomas, to spend the weekend, and they were preparing a fried chicken supper "when the doorbell rang. The man at the door asked if I were Rachel Davis DuBois. He asked the question a second time, making doubly clear I was the right person. Then he handed me a sheet of paper. It didn't seem very important to me at first. It was unsigned, so I asked what it was about. He said, a bit gruffly, "This is a subpoena from Senator McCarthy. It means you are to be in Washington by 2:30 next Monday and appear before the Senate Subcommittee on Government Operations"' (*ATSM*, 155).

Rachel felt sick. She knew of the McCarthy hearings and could not figure out why he wanted her to testify. Her first reaction was to contact her friend A. J. Muste, the national chair of the Fellowship of Reconciliation, a fellow Friend who Rachel held in high regard. Peg suggested Rachel call James Wechsler, editor of the *New York Post* who had previously undergone a McCarthy hearing. Rachel contacted Wechsler, and he suggested she secure the services of Washington, DC, attorney Joseph Rauh. Rachel made an appointment to see him that Sunday afternoon (*ATSM*, 155–156).

Rauh's advice to Rachel was simple: be direct, be honest, and talk about what she knew best for as long as she could. Rachel was *very* concerned that her very presence at the testimony was going to affect the work of the Workshop for Cultural Democracy (*ATSM*, 161). Rauh would be with her during the testimony, and she would be free to consult him as she answered questions. She did not have time to contact the Workshop Board.

This time, Rachel did not question her faith, she did not question her abilities, nor her politics. She was surrounded by friends and Friends, her sharing-caring communities who held her up in prayer.

On Monday, 8 June 1953, Rachel appeared before McCarthy and his committee, led by his chief counsel Roy Cohn. She was asked her name and to swear to tell the truth. She did not swear, as a Quaker takes no oath. She affirmed herself and intention to tell the truth. She was asked to explain her occupation, and she responded that she was Director of the Workshop for Cultural Democracy. When asked to explain, she told the committee, "It is an organization which works with groups of people in order to overcome the tensions in our country between people of different nationalities, religions, backgrounds, etc." (Transcript of McCarthy Testimony 1953, 1292). The committee asked about how the workshop was funded, to which she responded that it worked primarily with donations from individuals, churches, and community groups. She was asked to describe her work in Germany under the auspices of the US State Department, which she did, and then they hit her: "Have you ever been a member of the Communist Party?" "No." "Have you ever been a Communist?" "No. No good Quaker could become a member of the Communist party or any party which uses force and violence" (Transcript of McCarthy Testimony 1953, 1293).

Then there was confusion. Roy Cohn asked Rachel if she had been involved with the American Committee for the Protection of the Foreign Born. Rachel had heard of it, but she wasn't involved with the organization. Cohn kept asking questions about organizations she might have been involved with, but she had no recollection. Interspersed were questions, asked in many ways, if Rachel was a member of the Communist Party. She consistently responded in the negative, but it was Roy Cohn who persisted. Rachel finally said: " I am against the whole movement of communism [sic] because it is in line with the most negative forces in the world today" (1953, 1298).

And that was it. But Rachel was still concerned that her presence before McCarthy would have a negative bearing on the Workshop for Cultural Democracy. She was assured that there would be nothing in the newspapers or other media about her testimony, but word did leak out and a few organizations, one in the Bronx, another in Rochester, New York, canceled arrangements for Rachel to work with them (*ATSM*, 166). Business was slowing down but not stopped. In a sense, Rachel conquered McCarthy, though he tried to conquer her.

Everything I have written about so far implies the communicative value of folklore in education and education in folklore. For Rachel, getting to this place places her squarely in a comfort zone as an educator, advocate, Quaker, and guide. Her works are the seedbeds from which folklore and education are transplanted and grown. Those seeds survived the worst. This transplantation will be discussed and detailed in the chapter of conclusions where the past is truly prologue.

Notes

1. Joy and love permeate Rachel's writings. Based, in part, by the tenets of Quaker faith, it is a constant.
2. *Miscellaneous papers, Historical Society of Pennsylvania.*
3. "The Workshop for Cultural Democracy: A Fascinating Venture in Human Relations." 1945, Descriptive marketing pamphlet.
4. 1939. "Note" in Folk News 48(3).

References

Deafenbaugh, Linda. 2017. *Developing the Capacity for Tolerance Through Folklife Education.* Unpublished PhD diss., University of Pittsburgh.

DuBois, Rachel Davis. 1941a. "Intercultural Education and Democracy's Defense." *Friends Intelligencer,* February, pp. 70–72.

———. 1941b. "What Is Needed for Democracy's Defense?" *Friends Intelligencer,* February, pp. 69–70.

———. 1945. *Cultural Unity in the Making.* Reprint from Seventeenth Yearbook, California Association of Elementary Education Principals, Np.

———. 1950. *Neighbors in Action: A Manual for Local Leaders in Intergroup Relations.* New York: Harper & Brothers.

———. 1984. *(ATSM) All This and Something More: Pioneering in Intercultural Education.* Bryn Mawr: Dorrance.

Duncan, Ethel. 1945. *Democracy's Children.* New York: Hinds, Hayden, and Eldredge.

Harlam, Larry. 1950. "The *Parranda:*" "Report to the Workshop for Cultural Democracy". n.d./n.p.

Schwartz, Blanche. 1948. *Parranda and Program.* High Points.

Transcript of McCarthy Testimony [led by Roy Cohn]. 1953. https://www.senate.gov/artandhistory/generic/McCarthytranscripts.htm.

CHAPTER 9

Conclusions: The Past Is Prologue: Notes for Understanding Folklore and Education Considering the Pedagogy of Rachel Davis DuBois

While the *Parranda* enjoyed success on a local level, the Workshop for Cultural Democracy continued to be called into action nationally and internationally. Rachel continued teaching Intercultural Education at Columbia, and in 1945, the US Department of State hired the Workshop to conduct group conversations with World War II refugees in Germany (*ATSM*, p. 135).

Fellow Quakers, with a desire to learn more of their brethren interpersonally, also engaged the Workshop for Cultural Democracy (*ATSM*, 183–209). The staff at the Quaker-based Earlham College tried Workshop approaches to establish relations between its African American students and White students (*ATSM*, 239–254).[1]

Rachel through the Workshop worked with the Civil Rights Movement with Dr. Martin Luther King, Jr. (*ATSM*, 210–238). A group was founded, the Atlanta Dialogue, and Rachel maintained steady contact with its members until the 1970s.

Rachel moved back to her ancestral home in Woodstown, New Jersey, in 1976. According to biographer and fellow Friend George Crispin (personal communication 20 August 2016), Rachel never officially retired, nor was the Workshop officially dissolved. Rachel was 84 when she moved to her home called "Dawns Edge." She was beginning to experience health issues, including profound deafness, which obviously hindered conduct in Group Conversation and the Neighborhood-Home Festival. Although there are no records to the contrary, Rachel returned to the flora she loved so dearly and the spirituality that held her close in the hardest of times, such as her experience with the Service Bureau and the McCarthy hearings.

Rachel remained a member of the Woodstown Meeting, and on occasion, fellow Friend Chris Mahon would drive her to Philadelphia on AFSC business.

Rachel passed away on 30 March 1993. She was 101 years old and led an incredibly rich life of "blips" on her *longue durée*. As Montalto pointed out (1978), Rachel's life and works fell into the category of a "forgotten dream." Her publications rest for us to find in the archived journals, especially *The Friends Intelligencer* and *The Journal of Educational Sociology*. The books/manuals she published through Hines, Hayden, and Eldredge (1940), and Harper Brothers (1943, 1950) are no longer in print, but can be found through such services as Abe Books and Amazon. Biographer Nicholas Montalto now operates Diversity Dynamics, a group that uses much of Rachel's ideas to create solutions to issues of cultural diversity to businesses. Diana Selig is in the history department at Claremont College; George Crispin is a "gentleman farmer" who lives a quiet life in New Jersey, where on occasion he has facilitated Group Conversations (personal communication, 20 August 2016), and I own and operate Heritage Education Resources, a non-profit devoted to the provision of resource materials and services for those interested in heritage and cultural diversity (1997) where I conduct research on a variety of folklife-related projects, as well as documentary efforts of organizations devoted to development of human potential.[2]

Why is Rachel and her work a "forgotten dream?" There are a couple of possible reasons, some personal, and some professional. The fact of the matter, as I will be demonstrating, is that Rachel's work and the work of folklorists in education is supremely labor intensive, involving many responsibilities. There are logistics, content, presentation, and production of reports, materials, and funding applications. For most folklorists, and educators, too, this kind of work isn't the only kind of work to do. We all have other matters to answer to, and programs such as the ones Rachel designed and executed, and the ones folklorists are doing can be particularly overwhelming. Rather than create the kinds of channels for sustaining programs, they are more often than not "swept under the rug."

9 CONCLUSIONS: THE PAST IS PROLOGUE: NOTES FOR UNDERSTANDING...

Rachel, as I have been writing all along, was a maverick, a singular soul leaving a legacy for forwarding Intercultural Education in many directions, historically, socially, and spiritually. In these conclusions on folklore/folklife education and Intercultural Education, I will outline, compare, and contrast Rachel's work as it relates to folklore/folklife education, seeking common denominators and the differences between the two. This is to say there is no *one* approach. What I do say is that *if it weren't for folklore, there would be no Intercultural Education as Rachel designed it*. On the other side of the same coin, without Intercultural Education's forms and structures, folklore/folklife education, given its concern for customs, genres, expressions, and its mission as a social justice movement, would stumble, fall, and collect even more dust.

To recap Rachel's development, please allow the assistance of the following diagrams. Her goal was to develop tolerance which in today's terminology means "respect." Diagram 9.1 illustrates the first level of program

Diagram 9.1 The relationship of emotion, intellect, and social action to tolerance/sympathy/respect

Diagram 9.2 The interaction of invite, inform, incite, and influence and tolerance/sympathy/respect

design, the supply of experience in *emotional, intellectual, and social* terms [**Place Tolerance 7A**]. Diagram 9.2 shows the stages of program design for inviting community and school members, *informing* and *involving* one another with information on culture groups [**Place Tolerance 7B**].

Diagram 9.3 is an outgrowth of the work of Intercultural Education in answering the *wishes* of program process: the wish for recognition, the wish for response, the desire for new experience, and the sense of safety in cultural being [**Place Tolerance 7C**]. Diagram 9.4 shows the further interaction represented in Diagrams 9.1, 9.2, 9.3, and 9.5 shows everything put together to create a visual representation of a program that is circular, cyclical, and evolving [**Place Tolerance [D & E]**].

Rachel's work pre-date a scheme for determining what is considered a "best practice": http://www.besteducationpractices.org/what-is-a-best-practice/.[3] There are three levels of activity that lead to a best practice:

9 CONCLUSIONS: THE PAST IS PROLOGUE: NOTES FOR UNDERSTANDING... 123

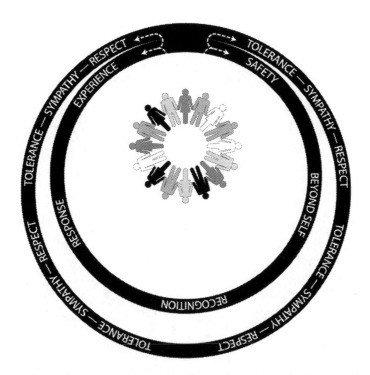

Diagram 9.3 Outgrown of the work of intercultural education in answering the wishes of recognition, response, new experience, safety, and outer experience

1. **Promising**: appears to result in positive outcomes not systematically evaluated;
2. **Validating**: the program has undergone rigorous evaluation and is deemed to result in a positive outcome; and
3. **Exemplary**: demonstrates replicability over time and space.

Rachel was able to explore and implement these three phases as a teacher, and then as a student and activist. Table 9.1 outlines this progression.

Rachel was working in fixed environments, the college, school, and home in which she constantly re-tooled her approach in order to fit the perceived need of schools and social settings as living organisms and laboratories, without sacrificing the taproot of her Concern to eradicate racism.

Diagram 9.4 Diagrams 9.1–9.3 in a cyclical motion

Table 9.1 From promising to exemplary practice in Rachel's work

Promising (Local)	Validating (Local and regional)	Exemplary (National)
Assembly at Woodbury High school (1925–1929)	Experimenting with Assembly and Group Conversation at Teacher's College and New York University (1929–1940)	Woodbury Plan (Assembly); Group Conversation; Neighborhood-Home Festival, Parranda (1938–1945)

In the course of her work, Rachel created "Learning Communities." Table 9.2. These groups were vital when it came to planning programs, as they kept Rachel aware of needs that would contribute to program design.

In Table 9.3 four themes describe the genealogy of Rachel's development from childhood to the creation of the Workshop for Cultural Democracy. Between 1895 and 1953 Rachel grew from a little girl with a

9 CONCLUSIONS: THE PAST IS PROLOGUE: NOTES FOR UNDERSTANDING... 125

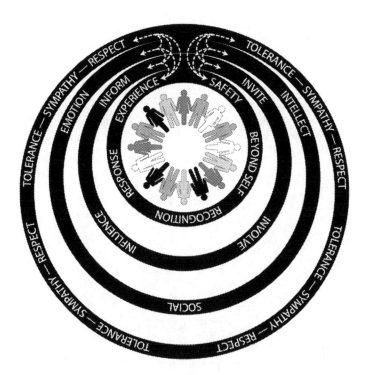

Diagram 9.5 Diagrams 9.1 through 9.4 put together to show the entire process behind intercultural education

Table 9.2 Learning communities in Rachel's work

Family	School	Community
Immigrant state (First Wave/ Second Wave)	Students' graduates Dominant languages spoken Curriculum Ethnic Make-Up Teacher training Representation (Union, P.T.A. Administrative staff)	Ethnicities Socio-economics Fraternal/civic orders Representation (religious groups, law enforcement, clubs, vendors, businesses)

Table 9.3 Rachel's life themes and events

I didn't know what I didn't know	Childhood discovery of ethnic difference	Poems/letters for Bill Williams (African American), Opera with Joe Pignatelli	1895–1920
Roll and Rock with the shifting sand	College, finding Concern, Woodbury, graduate school, Service Bureau, program development and testing	Dreaming Ahead; creation of Assembly; Graduate school, program development and testing (emotion, intellect, social action); five wishes (recognition, response, experience, security, experience beyond the self); Service Bureau, Americans All radio; Intercultural Education and politics, forced resignation from the Service Bureau	1910–1940
"I am nothing, thou art all"	Heard seminar	Losing ego (do you want to win the battle, or do you want to win the war?); Monday night group with Heard alumni in New York	1941
Sharing-Caring	Workshop for Cultural Democracy	Intercultural Education Workshop; Workshop for Cultural Democracy; Parranda; IRS 501(c)(3) accepted	1942, 1945, 1946, 1950

hint of awareness of cultural diversity and spirituality to her Concern and pacifist advocacy for human rights by way of programming, advanced schooling, the establishment of the Service Bureau for Intercultural Education (SBIE), and the birth of the Workshop for Cultural Democracy.

Through Heard, Rachel began to develop and hone the tools necessary for disengaging her ego from what was going on in her programs, but her heart never left her sleeve. She applied the mantra Heard gave her (I am nothing, thou art all) in such a way that she arrived at a consciousness that she realized she had been questing for since she began her work in 1924. And it was Rachel's spirituality and emotion that infused so much of her work, and that is something that sets her work apart from the work of folklorists in educational environments today. With her, those qualities contributed to much of the friction that caused her resignation from the Service Bureau.

Table 9.4 outlines the goals of folklore and education and approaches to Intercultural Education. This table is an extrapolation of thought in folklife education because, to confirm Lynne Hamer's understanding (Hamer 2000, 45), that there is very little literature that explores the

Table 9.4 Goals of folklore and education and approaches to intercultural education

Goals of Folklore & Education (Bowman and Hamer, 2011, 12–13)	Approaches to Intercultural Education (DuBois, 1925, 1943, 1945, 1950)
1. Helps students and teachers identify and value their own and familiar folk groups and their vernacular and everyday artistic expressions	1. Work with students, community members, teachers, and staff to identify cultural representatives to present culture and contributions to American life
2. With 1 and a folklorist's perspective, students see the importance of familiar heroes and local events	2. Engage 1 in recognizing contributions to American life in self and other
3. Folklore and Education encourages critical thinking about various types of cultural expression	3. 2 along with study of cultural contributions
4. F&E re-centers authority outside institutions	4. Encourage community examination and interaction
5. Work is inherently collaborative in and out of the classroom	5. Work together for cultural sharing and evaluation

underpinnings of folklore education. We do programs, and there are plenty of them. There does not appear to be comprehensive opportunities to talk about folklife education work.[4] This table outlines suggestions of what folklife education is built on. It forms the basis of an approach to the work of folklife education (Bowman and Hamer 2011, 12–13).

What this table and the others show is that folklife education today is easily blended into the program of Intercultural Education developed by Rachel in the 1920s through the 1950s. Programs are tools for consciousness raising, promoting tolerance, and appreciation. They build into what William A. Wilson (2006) calls a "value center," a deep pool of shared beliefs that goes even deeper than our *understanding* of what constitutes "culture." The value center is a part of any group, and it requires meeting stereotypes head-on, admitting prejudice, interacting with those we are prejudiced against, and sharing experience of the Other with self and others. Tweaking and re-tooling within the value center consists of re-tooling opinion through a reflection of the Self in relation to the Other and emerging on the "same page" where self and Other can share differences and likenesses in the spirit of cooperation. This is similar to Heard's identification of the rungs on the ladder to consciousness: enlightenment and union.

There are other differences between Rachel's thought and Hamer's analysis. One difference has to do with *function*. Hamer's analysis reflects a need for the use of folklore to create a sensitized and informed class of teaching professionals. Rachel's thought reflects what I call her *romantic functionalism*, in which the parts and pieces of her programs are put back together to embrace and reflect goodness and love amid Others and all of their (and our) cultural trials. Hamer's teachers are more clinical in approach. Rachel's participants, she hoped, would emerge with love in their hearts. Both, however, see folklore as a great equalizer. We are different, but we are united through our value centers.

Intercultural Education and Folklife education are for anyone who is interested in the complexities of heritage and cultural diversity (Rosenberg 1997).[5] Historically, each field has been applied in institutionalized settings, including schools and museums. To be involved, one seeks out a willing partner, such as the "Y" or a school or museum. Folklore and Education has grown from a "glorified dog and pony show" to a potentially legitimate insertion into an education environment's own programs. For Rachel, she had no problem with this as she was a seasoned classroom teacher and community presenter.

Rachel left an approach to cultural competence that the folklorist working in education can apply. For the programs folklorists in education design there is a need to figure out time-management, alternative ways to determine graduates K-16 and their mentors' needs. For the folklorist who wishes to do this work, he or she must acknowledge education environments and fit in accordingly. The whole of the school outweighs the whole of folklife education. While the school or other education agencies might want a folklife component, it is our responsibility to make sure our work fits with their mission and structure.

An approach to folklife education can utilize the architecture of Rachel's programs, the emotional, the intellectual, and the social, the wishes for recognition, response, experience, security, experience beyond the self, and the "4-Is" The role of a visiting tradition bearer today is perhaps more expansive than it was with Rachel's programs, but tradition bearers were found in the community and the family in her work and in ours. We still must work through issues of time, presenting lessons in sync with the teacher's arrangement of the day, the function of the school, and its systems for implementation included in its architecture and overall schedule.

Rachel has laid a groundwork for folklore/folklife education. As bricoleur, she has recounted a long and arduous journey that can't be abandoned. As a romantic functionalist, she truly believed in her programs and their capacity for encouraging knowledge, joy, and love. Rachel is Intercultural Education's and Folklore Education's bricoleur (Shukla, personal communication 24 November 2018). She has gathered the essentials and the fragments of her memory and has given us a crafted final narrative (assemblage) for us to use as we learn the needs of the environments and people we are to work with including tradition bearers, teachers, principals, students, and families. Rachel's practice and thought are her contribution to a pedagogy for folklife education from which we can exact best practices.

Linda Deafenbaugh's dissertation, "Developing the Capacity for Tolerance Through Folklife Education" (2017, University of Pittsburgh), is relatively close to what Rachel set out to do. It is an exploration of a model for encouraging a group of high school students in a Pittsburgh school to explore their cultural differences and similarities and those in a space-place area of the city, using "ethnographic methods … during a semester-long elective course, "Cultural Anthropology and Digital Media." The study "investigated student learning from the students' perspective," … focusing "on how student learning about cultural processes via *The Standards for Folklife Education*," (1997) designed by Diane Sidener that developed students' capacity for social tolerance" (pp. iv-v) utilizing a progressive set of steps toward content and performance standards bringing a student to examining the self in tradition and into describing cultural activity at home and in the community. This chart presents two major content and performance standards and what areas of Rachel's approach matches to them. These can relate to students as well as those who participate in Group Conversation and the Neighborhood-Home Festival (Sidener, 16) (Table 9.5).

The Capacity for Tolerance model is a bottom-up approach to student learning. "It illustrates how the study of cultural processes via this folklife education approach helped students gain more complex understandings about the interlocked nature of cultural similarities and differences" (Deafenbaugh, iv).

The approach relies on ethnographic practice, and on what Rachel identified as the emotion, intellectual, and social components (see Chaps. 4 and 5). The students, like the adults and students Rachel worked with, started their work by exploring their lives as members of a folk group with traditional practices alive in their communities and families (the "me"), and from there, they moved to explore the similarities and differences in the lives of those in the geographic area surrounding their school (the "we"). Throughout the course, the Pittsburgh students wrote and talked about their experiences and their analyses and understandings of them as they related to themselves and others.

Table 9.5 Comparison of folklife standards that are applicable to Rachel's three elements

Folklife content standard	Folklife performance standard	Rachel's element
1. Understanding folk groups and how they relate to individuals, to each other and to larger cultural groups	1A: students compare beliefs and practices that express and/or shape worldview of their own and other folk groups	Emotion: exposure of self and others
	1C: students identify their own cultural traditions, describing their own cultural identity	A continuation of emotion, with cultural information on participants woven throughout.
	1D: students investigate the interrelations among folk groups and between folk groups and larger cultural groups	Intellectual: learning about other people Social: meeting people to learn about people
2. Recognizing the range of experience encompassed by the many forms of folklife expression	Students explain processes by which traditions are maintained, altered, lost, and revived	Social and intellectual: exploration of contributions groups make to American life

The students in Pittsburgh were engaged as Rachel's participants were. They were exposed emotionally to a world of their own and of others. They embarked on an intellectual journey into the cultures ethnographically. Socially, their understandings of similarities and differences brought them closer together as a sharing-caring group.

Students in the Capacity for Tolerance project had something to share with the wishes described by Rachel. The course provided opportunities for recognition, a response to the world, new experiences in meeting themselves and others, safety in being able to express themselves, and a chance to be involved in something beyond themselves. They engaged in an exercise of coming together and distancing themselves in a way that they would be able to come together as a community with the capacity for tolerance. This was a rare project, one that had the potential for becoming a best practice. But the project did not last beyond Deafenbaugh's time at the school. Although the teachers she worked with embraced and participated in the project's concept and execution, they chose not to continue the class due to other pressing responsibilities (personal communication, Deafenbaugh, n.d.).

Rachel's programs and folklorists' projects were meticulous in design and execution, based on a common *hope for respect for others through folk-*

lore. There are differences, reflected in our attitude toward the work. Rachel had no problem wearing her heart on her sleeve, especially when she had to deal with the Service Bureau's board who felt she was quixotic and out of step with the education endeavor. The SBIE board was misogynist and felt their approach to intercultural education was the *right* method. What folklorists working in education seem to be showing is there currently is no *correct* way of doing the work. Unfortunately, wearing one's heart on his or her sleeve in this day and age can seem counter to the tasks at hand. Such behavior could be construed as "unprofessional" and unsuitable in a formal environment.

Another factor that gives Rachel's design a distinctive flavor is her use of the dramaturgic. Given her experience in her telling of jokes to gain acceptance from her college classmates, her elocution lessons, and involvement in theater while in college, she engaged dramaturgy in her classes and in her programs, In the first act, Rachel employed the structure of drama's rehearsal in preparing educators, students, tradition bearers, and communities for the second major act, the assembly, group conversation/ the Neighborhood-Home Festival, and the *Parranda*. The third act was evaluative. She encouraged looking in the mirror and walking in the shoes of others. Out of this she hoped for tolerance, the respect of cultural difference through gathering information, inviting and involving educators, students, parents, promoters of social justice, folklorists, sociologists, and community members in the work, and hopefully influencing the attitudes of all involved, encouraging the heart and the mind.

Instead of drama, folklorists deal with ethnography in the creation of programs. We set out to explore and document peoples and traditions in action which leads to the creation of projects highlighting tradition-based peoples and communities. Informing, inviting, involving, and influencing guides how we create folklife education residencies and short-term programs. We, like Rachel hope for tolerance, respect. But rather than jump into the work, we step back to learn and understand so we can work with interested parties on programs. Description, rather than drama, informs our designs.

Ethnography is etic in the sense that we use it to explore and explain culture at work. Rachel's works are more emic because of her preparations and executions of her programs which were highly inclusionary. She made that happen in the contexts of the school and community. Deafenbaugh's study and program straddles emic and etic (Pike 1955). She wanted her students to engage themselves as "ordinary people doing extraordinary things" using principled ethnography, looking inward and with skill, the students were able to stretch into the etic, explaining community and exploring its dynamic, just as an educational sociologist would do.

The fields of education history and the nature of folklore's study is dynamic and perhaps, traumatic. Why might this be so? With the former, the blips on its screen are well spent and weathered with time. As for the latter, folklore, it has gone through many revolutions to get to where it is today as the quest for understanding tradition and its manifold constructs for education's purposes.[6] The same can be said for folklife education and educational sociology. The genealogy of Rachel's field, Educational Sociology, stretches to the early 1900s, and the field of folklore education's notice goes back to 1976 with the first folklore and education programs, though the first folklore studies go back to 1888[7] with the establishment of the American Folklore Society. We are just catching up.

While Rachel's programs are best practices, folklife education has yet to establish itself as a best practice; its practitioners are on the constant lookout for the new and usable in its field. Folklife education as a practice is a *validating practice*. People working in the field are constantly developing new approaches, often not looking back to see what has been done. The question of "what works" is very much in the air, but folklorists working in education often times do not have the time to explore "what works" when it comes to our storehouse of practice.

As our field goes around and around, we have identified many arenas for practice. Ours is in a kind of identity crisis as we seek out what we *think is best*. Through "trial and terror" we have actually concluded, that like Rachel's programs, folklife education can be practiced in multiple environments. But just because we might not have total success, say with schools, those places do not deserve to be abandoned. We are armed with the tools of folklore but not as much as what we can borrow from a teacher or community leaders, or health care professionals. Communication between all parties must be mandatory. Talking with one another (face to face) is vital when it comes to learning needs and working through those needs. Just as important is for us to get "a feel" for the classroom or education environment we are to work with (this includes the teacher *and* the students, their families and communities). While we have a clutch of results, one remains. We need to continue to learn the deep world view, the value center of the school/environment and figure out, with the teacher/curator/tradition bearer the center in terms of what the culture bearer wants to share.

Folklife education is hard work that requires the donning a variety of hats. We have the folklorist's hat that we use to identify tradition bearers and representatives we can work with. Then we have the educator's hat, the one we use to design lessons. Third is a blend of folklorist and presenter. And to top everything off, we have the hats of the librarian and the guidance counselor serving as resources and as listeners to needs. We have to be able to switch hats "on the fly," because these hats need to be at the ready when a situation arises so quickly. Folklife education is hard work, not only in the application of hats; it is a large investment of time and energy. Programs require more than a "cut out-get out" approach. They require constant tending, a giving and taking of expertise, and a concern for inclusivity for all involved. Folklife education is challenging as we try to be nimble with the value center of the education environments and our discipline. From 7:30 a.m. to 3:30 p.m., the value center of the school is first and foremost in the many workings of both the school plant and the school's citizenry. If folklorists working in education are not careful, our works will remain under the title of "add-ons" which, no matter what we do, is a threat to the balance of the educational day.

It only looks messy.

If we apply Rachel's model to our works, we are in no way compromising the fields of education, of folklore in general and folklife education specifically. Rather, we are adding a deepened human element, an intense commitment to tradition, tradition bearers, and their relationship to a world at-large. We must add to that a commitment a deep and continued respect for the teacher and his or her craft, something we cannot override. We strive for these commitments, firming them through the various types of training we do in preparation for units. But as we are not necessarily teachers, teachers are not necessarily folklorists. This doesn't mean we all are ignorant of cultural realities. We give, we're open to taking. We strive to stand firm on the same page. To do that, we might ask ourselves (1) why am I doing folklife education? (2) why is education (especially in education environments) important? and (3) "what can I bring to the page?"

Earlier, in describing Rachel's use of an empathetic spirit in her teaching at Glassboro (Chap. 4), I wrote that in the classroom she used what she liked when she was a student and that she didn't use that which she didn't like when she was a student. There are going to be some of us who had a wonderful experience in school, and it colors our engagements. Then there are others who didn't have a positive K-12 school experience, and through our love of folklore and folkloristics, we're able to share that care over the skull drudgery of our classroom experience. We want somehow to make things right, and through folklife education, we hopefully can provide a condition of care in those we interact with, especially those who hate or hated school.

But that doesn't answer the question about why education is important. It all depends on what we call "education." As folklorists, we know that education takes place in a wide arrangement of situations and contexts. Through folklife education, it is the tradition bearer's ability to share his or her education outside of the traditional education environment, demonstrating the importance of looking in and scoping out when it comes to the benefits of knowledge, whatever it may be.

So, what can we bring to the page? Opportunities for looking at the power of folklore and its effects on education, no matter how we define education. One of the reasons why I like Lawrence Cremin's definition of education as "the deliberate, systematic, and sustained effort to transmit, evoke, or acquire knowledge, attitudes, values, skills, or sensibilities as well as any outcomes of that effort" (Cremin 1976, viii). It leaves the field wide open when it comes to the "how" of learning. Perhaps one of the drawbacks of folklife education today is it is (and has always been) genre-based, focusing on the power and beauty of making things. We live in a world today that is in a cultural imbalance as war rips into the human core. Education as a formal read/write/arithmetic has been upended physically with the shortage of places for the R's can take place. And that's not only in the middle eastern countries. A close look at Marjory Stoneman Douglas, Sandy Hook, Columbine, and elsewhere in the United States has undermined the one thing that is important to the education venture: safety.

For what Rachel says in the design of programs, it seems that, for folklorists working in education, much is left unsaid. We use all the elements of Rachel's works in our work, but there seems to be a kind of resistance when we talk about the EQ and SQ (see Chap. 6). If we don't identify with Rachel's construct, are we suggesting our approaches are more scholarly, more objective, more in tune with education's and folklore's functions today? Are we suggesting that Rachel's works represent some sort of "Triviality Barrier?" (Sutton-Smith 1970) that only we can get over? In doing this, we might be giving Rachel the short end of the stick, while she created a field that covered so much ground, both in terms of the EQ, the IQ, and the SQ. And she encourages introspection as we set out to do our work. Because Rachel's work is almost virtually unknown, it is something we can correct by giving it a place at the table as we develop and describe our works.

Rachel left us powerful guidance and in order to move into the future with effective mindset and techniques, we can embrace certain points that have been standing the test of time for nearly a century. These points developed in many settings and periods.

We can trust Rachel. She worked to her utmost for decades to develop methods that achieved goals that overcame intractable problems where many others had failed. She emerged from a unique time and place that gave her certain human characteristics that few have had. (She wasn't working to get tenure.) She conceived her Concern that remained her concern for the rest of her long life.

Rachel laid down a granite foundation for folklore in education utilizing the stone blocks quarried by John Dewey and a few other pioneers in educational sociology.

When we emerge from the chrysalis of graduate school, we are eager to fly and show the world our wings, sometimes ignoring and/or condescending to those who carved out the path we follow. Disregarding this foundation builds a house on sand, a house which may have superficial likenesses to folklore, but which contains little substance and achieves little of importance. Folklife Education is difficult, requires serious thought, is very work intensive, and requires that we check our ego at the door. Otherwise, we are in danger of becoming formulaic and superficial. Keeping the guiding principles keeps our stone foundation while allowing the freedom of creativity in shaping programs.

This is our responsibility as people uniquely trained in a very special field, to ameliorate the severe damage to our society currently under attack. This is a solemn duty and can be our joy. We have a key to unlock much negativity in our society.

The past is prologue—we need to salute it. It's not about "me"; it's about "we."

Notes

1. "Rachel Davis DuBois's Report of Her Residence on the Earlham College Campus," 9 September 1971–1 December 1971.
2. These include (1) documentation of school life between 1915 and 1931 in Bloomington, Indiana; (2) work with the Fuller Center for Housing, a radicalized offshoot of Habitat for Humanity; and (3) the creation of an archive for Tuxedo Park Baptist Church whose records go back to its founding in 1902.

3. Thanks are due to Dr. Linda Deafenbaugh for sharing this site.
4. *The Journal of Folklore and Education*, a peer review journal from the National Network for Folk Arts in Education, could address this lack, but it has yet to include it in its theme-related design.
5. This is the stated mission of Heritage Education Resources' Articles and By-laws.
6. See Thomas Kuhn: *The Structure of Scientific Revolutions*. 1962, 1972. Chicago: University of Chicago Press.
7. See Sharon Celsor Hughes's report on Folklore and Education programming. Available from Jan Rosenberg (janrosenberg@att.net).

References

Bowman, Paddy and Lynne Hamer (eds.) 2011. *Through the Schoolhouse Door: Folklore, Community, Curriculum*. Logan, UT: Utah State University Press.

Cremin, Lawrence. 1976. *Traditions of American Education*. New York: Basic Books.

Hamer, Lynne. 2000. "Folklore in Schools and Multicultural Education: Toward Institutionalizing Noninstitutional Knowledge." *Journal of American Folklore* 113 (447): 44–69.

Pike, Kenneth L. 1955. *Language in Relation to a Unified Theory of the Structure of Human Behavior*. Glendale, CA: Summer Institute of Linguistics.

Rosenberg, Jan. 1997 "An Eclectic Schoolteacher: Dorothy Howard as Applied Folklorist." *Children's Folklore Review*. Vol. 30. Pp. 61–68.

Sidener, Diane, ed. 1997. *Standards for Folklife Education: Integrating Language Arts, Social Studies, Arts and Science Through Student Traditions and Culture*. Immaculata, PA: The Pennsylvania Folklife Education Committee.

Sutton-Smith, Brian. 1970. "Psychology of Childlore: The Triviality Barrier." *Western Folklore* 29 (1): 1–8.

Wilson, William A. 2006. *The Marrow of Human Experience*. Ed. Jill Terry Rudy. Logan, UT: Utah State University Press.

Epilogue

Rachel's Award: Woodbury's Reward

In July 2016 I was in Philadelphia following up on some research of Rachel's works at the Historical Society of Pennsylvania. I stayed at a hotel that was next to a trophy shop, and I had a thought: would it be possible for the school where Rachel started the Intercultural Education movement to put up a plaque honoring her and the school? It was just a thought, maybe a nice one.

I contacted the school, Woodbury Junior/Senior High School, and spoke with the principal, Mr. Eder Joseph. He was interested in the idea and we made an appointment to discuss it later in the week. I prepared a binder of information relating to Rachel, the school, and the Assembly program which she started at Woodbury in 1925, and began to get excited about this plan I hatched.

Woodbury is about 20 miles from Philadelphia. On a hot day I made the trip through cluttered Jersey towns and found the school. The first thing I noticed was the cornerstone for the school, dated 1908. This was the very building in which Rachel taught. I wondered what it was like for her to climb the short set of stairs into the staid front of the school. The front office was open and I asked a person at the front desk if Mr. Joseph was available. The school interior was under renovations, and I was told he was checking up on progress. Invited to take a seat, I held my binder and waited. After 15 minutes, Mr. Joseph appeared, and after face-to-face introductions, we sat down for business. Would the school be interested in a small plaque honoring Rachel and the school for its pioneering in Intercultural Education?

Mr. Joseph was interested and positive. He took the binder and told me he would speak with the school district superintendent and get back to me. He then took me on a tour of the building to show me the renovations. The school exterior, he pointed out, would look the same as it did in 1908. The interior, however, was to be outfitted with new tile, new classroom designs, and a more welcoming media center. Given my interest in school architecture, this was an unexpected treat.

I left the school feeling positive. There just might be a plaque. I took photographs of the school exterior, and headed back to Philadelphia by making a roundabout trip about the town and outskirts of Woodbury, thinking I just might see the agricultural landscape that was Rachel's home. After passing through a town outfitted for tourists with coffee shops and shops, I got out on to the country roads, and admired the greenery, in spite of what my car said were 90 + degree heat (it was also incredibly humid—that's July for you).

As I drove, I wondered what Rachel would make of Woodbury and the school. At home when I conducted online research, I learned that, indeed, the population has changed. It is no more a matter of Black and White. According to the 2010 Census, Woodbury was home to Whites 66.01%, 4.91% African Americans, 0.23% Native Americans, 0.28% Asian, Hispanic 10.66% (*Wikipedia, 31 May 2019*).

At school there are changes as well. Woodbury Junior/Senior High School, home of the Thundering Herd, is diverse in its population. Of the 748 students, 43% are African American, 36% White, 16% Hispanic, and 2% Asian (www.woodburysch.com). Students are offered access to individual computers in each classroom, and any student can take an Advanced Placement (AP) class despite his or her grade point average. The school uses a STEM approach—Science-Technology-Engineering-Math in its whole of course offerings, and it was recognized for its social-directed mission where all students are welcomed and affirmed in classes and the school community (personal communication, Cohen, 16 May 2019).

When returned to home to Bloomington, I didn't hear from Mr. Joseph. I didn't expect to as the school renovations had to be completed by the end of August, and the superintendent surely had much on his plate. And so I carried on with my research and writing on Rachel.

In early 2017 I received an email from an Edward Murphy. He was in charge of pupil and personnel development for the Woodbury schools, and he was on the school district's minority task force. He explained that Mr. Joseph had left Woodbury, leaving him a pile of unfinished business which included my binder. He was definitely interested, not only in having a plaque but in having an award for a teacher whose work reflected Rachel's spirit, and creating a small archive featuring works related to Rachel. As they say in my adopted South, I was *gobsmacked*! Mr. Murphy and I spoke on a number of occasions, enough to be on a first-name basis, and he told me that the Rachel Davis DuBois Award would have its first recipients in June 2017. There would be a small plaque, and the small library was in the works. In May he asked me to come to Woodbury to present the award on 4 June to two Woodbury personnel, social worker Gloria Good and classroom aide Aquanetta Allen. I couldn't make the trip, so Ed asked me to record a brief message to accompany the giving of the award. My recording recognized Rachel and Woodbury as pioneers in Intercultural Education and thanked Good and Allen for their service. Today, the award is still given through the district's Minority Task Force. Rachel would be either pleased or humbled.

Grave Marker, Salem County, New Jersey: Inscription Racheal [sic] DuBois, Mother of Intercultural Education

Index[1]

A
Addams, Jane, vi
Adventures in Intercultural Education (DuBois), 32, 69, 79, 89
African Americans, 17, 43, 65
  education for, vi, 23, 42, 66
  farmers, 21
  Rachel's empathy for, 3, 23, 42–44, 57–59, 65, 66
  segregation, 57
All This and Something More: Pioneering in Intercultural Education (DuBois), 12, 23, 32
American Committee for the Protection of the Foreign Born, 116
American education, 13
Americanization, 34
  See also Assimilation; Diversity; Immigrants
Americanizing Our Foreign Born (Rugg), 75n1
American Jewish Committee (AJC), 3, 80, 81, 83, 93n1
American Legion, 70
Americans All-Immigrants All (CBS), vii, 4, 26, 78, 88
American School of the Air (ASA), 26, 88
Anderson, Joe, 11, 13
Anthropology, 22, 23, 80, 96
Arkansas, 70
Assemblage, 129
Assembly, 2, 107, 110
Assembly Program, 23
Assimilation
  Americanization, 83
  in education, 83
  melting pot, America as, 83
  See also Diversity; Immigrants
Atlanta Dialogue, 119
Attitudinal scale, Neumann's, 79

---
[1] Note: Page numbers followed by 'n' refer to notes.

B
Bacon Academy, 46
Balch Institute, 11, 12
Baldwin, Karen, 27
Balee, Susan, 41
Baptist schools, 19
Barrens, Pine, 44
Behaviorism, 97
Benedict, Ruth, 23, 30, 80
Benedictine Silence, 99
Boas, Franz, 23, 30, 80
Bowman, Paddy, 27, 28, 127
Bricoleur, 41, 128
Brown, A.R. Radcliffe, 30
Bucknell University, 60n2
Build Together Americans: Adventures in Intercultural Education For the Secondary School (DuBois), 32, 33

C
Capacity for tolerance, 109
Carney, Mabel, 81
Catskills, 26
CBS, *see* Columbia Broadcasting System
Chance, Harold, 95
Child saving movement, vi
Christ Jesus, 14, 16
Clinchy, Everett, 80, 81
Cohn, Roy, 116
Coles, Wilma, 19, 46, 51
Columbia Broadcasting System (CBS), 4, 26, 88
Columbia University (Teacher's College), 4, 29, 63, 75n1, 78
Committee on Race Relations, 63
Communist Party, 116
Community of tolerance, 68
"Concern," vi, 17
Congressional American Folklife Preservation Chapter of 1976, 22

Cremin, Lawrence, 5, 18, 21, 83, 134
Crispin, George A., 4, 14–16, 34, 85, 119, 120
Cultural democracy
 defined, 106
 demonstrations, 114
 Workshop for Cultural Democracy, vii, 2, 4, 8, 36, 105–117, 119, 124
 world unity, 108
 See also Parranda (intercultural party)
Culture, *see* Immigrants; *individual groups*; Intercultural Education
Culture shock, 56

D
Davis, Carol, 35
Davis, Ed, 34, 35
Davis Farm, 48
Davis, grandfather and grandmother, 19, 46
Davis, Walter, 49n1
Dawn's Edge, 13
Deafenbaugh, Linda, 129
Democracy, 89, 105–117
 See also Cultural democracy
Democracy's Children (Duncan, Thomas), 108
Dewey, John, 3, 13, 20, 46, 97, 135
Diversity
 assimilation, 83
 attitudes towards, 32
 within individual groups, 83
 See also Intercultural Education; Race relations; Segregation
Dramaturgic, 131
Dramaturgic approach, 55
'Dream ahead,' 64
Dreaming Ahead, 3, 96, 106
DuBois, Nathan Steward, 54

DuBois, Rachel, *see* Rachel
Duncan, Ethel, 108
Durlach, Teresa Mayer, 80

E
Early schooling, 46
Education
  behaviorism, 97
  child centered, 3
  defined, 18, 28, 30
  DuBois, Rachel (*see under* Rachel)
  field trips, 8, 113
  Folklore and Education, 8, 12, 13, 24–28, 117, 119–135
  Learning Communities, 68
  Office of Education, vii, 4, 88
  pedagogy, 5, 18, 28–31, 81, 119–135
  Progressive, 3, 13, 20, 82, 83
  Service Bureau for Intercultural Education, vii, 2, 4, 8, 34, 35, 69, 77–92, 106, 107, 124
  social studies, 20, 63
  vs. tradition, 45, 46, 134
  See also Education Sociology; Intercultural Education; Teachers
Education Sociology, 5, 6, 23, 28–31, 78, 85, 87, 97, 111, 132, 135
Educational Sociology (Kulp), 5, 6, 28–32, 70, 78, 80, 85, 87, 97, 111, 120
Educational Weekly, 30
Emotion, 3, 66, 67
Empathy, 99
Englewood school, 80
Enlightenment, 105
Ephraim, Miriam, 69
Ethnic groups, 43
Ethnicity, 4, 12, 58, 66, 83, 85

See also Diversity; Immigrants; *individual groups*; Race relations
Evolution, 69, 96, 97, 99

F
Faith and practice, 42
Farming, 17, 47
Finkelstein, Barbara, 6
Florida, 70
Folklife education, viii, 1
Folklore, v
  "American folklife," 22
  Assembly (*see* Woodbury Unified Assembly Plan)
  challenges of folklorists, 133
  Congressional American Folklife Preservation Chapter of, 22
  defined, 24
  folkdance, 22
  folklore and education, 8, 12, 13, 24–28, 117, 119–135
  folksong, 26, 85
Forgotten Dream, The; A History of the Intercultural Education Movement 1924–1941 (Montalto), 33
Fox, George, 14–16, 18, 97
Freud, Sigmund, vi, 29
Friends (Quakers), *see* Society of Friends
From Me to We: Three Early Twentieth Century Educators and the Development of Folklore and Education (Rosenberg), 34
Functionalism, 30

G
Get Together Americans (GTA) (DuBois), 32, 33, 93n3
Glassboro High School, 20, 54
Grange, 48

Group Conversation, vii, 1, 2, 4, 14, 24, 34, 35, 78, 85–87, 90–92, 101, 102, 105, 109, 110, 112, 113, 119, 120, 129, 131
Gulley, Philip, 15, 42, 55

H
Haines, Beulah, 51
Hamer, Lynne, 126–128
Hamm, Thomas D., 15
Heard, Gerald Fitzgerald, vii, 4, 36, 95–102, 103n1, 105, 106, 124, 127
Hicks, Elias, 15
[H]istorical biography, 6
History of education, v
Homogeneity, 17
    See also Diversity
Howard, Dorothy, 25, 28
Howard University, 58
Hull House, vi
Human Nature and Conduct (Dewey), 97
Huxley, Aldous, 96

I
Immigrants
    Americans All-Immigrants All (CBS), vii, 4, 26, 78, 88
    assimilation of, vi
    cultural exchange between (*see* Cultural democracy)
    by population, 59
    See also Diversity; *individual groups*; Race relations; Segregation
Indiana, 70
"Indigenous teacher", 26
Integration, 20, 28, 115
    See also Assimilation; Segregation
Intellect, 3, 66, 67
Intelligence Quotient(IQ), v, 19, 20, 29, 32, 80, 134

Intercultural Education, vi, 17
    components, vii, 101
    cultural democracy (*see* Cultural democracy)
    Folklore and Education, 126
    lack of, viii
    leaders, training course for, 35
    Parranda (intercultural party), 2, 119
    programs, development of, vii, 63–74, 122, 127
    Rachel's dissertation on, 32–34, 69, 79, 85, 89
    reactions to, 73
    Service Bureau, 2, 4, 34, 35, 69, 77–92, 106, 107, 124
    summer camps for, 26
    Workshop for Cultural Democracy, vii, 2, 4, 106, 115, 124
    See also Education Sociology; Folklore
Intercultural Education Workshop, 106
Internal Revenue Service (IRS), 106
IQ, *see* Intelligence Quotient
IRS, *see* Internal Revenue Service
Italians, 43

J
Jack, Mahon, 35, 120
Jersey Devil, 44
Jim Crow, vii, 2
JPS 165, 109
Judaism
    American Jewish Committee(AJC), 3, 80, 81
    in Rachel's early life, 44
    religion *vs.* culture, 3, 35, 83
Judaism as a Civilization (Kaplan), 84
Junior High School (JHS) 165, 109

K

Kaplan, Mordecai, 84
Katz, Michael B., 19, 31
Kilpatrick, William, 78
King, Martin Luther Jr., Dr., 119
Kingdom of Heaven, 48
Kuhn, Thomas S., v
Kulp, Daniel, II, 29, 78–80, 87, 107
Kurke, George, 109

L

LaVerne College, 96, 98
Learning Communities, 124
Liberation and Enlightenment, 100
Local Learning: The National Network for Folk Arts in Education, 28
Living the Quaker Way (Gulley), 15
Lomax, Alan, 25

M

Mahon, Chris, 35, 120
Malinowski, Bronislaw, 30
Martha Schofield School, 2, 56
Schofield School, 56
Maslow, Abraham, 44
McCarthy, Senator, 115
McKinley, William, 47
Mead, Margaret, 23, 30
Meditation, vii, 36, 98, 99, 101, 102
Methodist, 45
Mezger, M.L., 33
Montalto, Nicholas, 14, 31, 33, 120
Mount Holyoke College, 51
Muste, A. J., 115
Mysticism, 96

N

National Endowment for the Arts (NEA), 27, 71
Nationalism, 65
See also Assimilation; Immigrants
Neighborhood-Home Festival, vii, 1, 2, 4, 24, 78, 86, 87, 101, 105–107, 110, 120, 129, 131
Neighbors in Action (NIA) (DuBois), 32, 33
Neumann, George, 32, 65, 70, 79
New Jersey, 2, 13, 17, 19, 25, 42, 44, 54, 57, 59, 63, 80, 85, 106, 119, 120
See also Glassboro High School
New York University (NYU), 4, 23, 29, 32, 69, 78, 79, 87

O

Office of Education, vii, 4, 88
Oklahoma, 70
Our Town (Wilder), 6

P

Pacifism, 17, 55
See also Quakers
Parents Association, 110
Parent Teacher Association (PTA), 33
Parranda (intercultural party), viii, 1, 24, 105–117, 131
Payne, Edward George, 29
PEA, *see* Progressive Education Association
Peace Testimony of 1660, 6, 16
Pedagogy, 5, 8, 12, 17, 18, 21, 28–31, 55, 57, 68, 81, 119–135
See also Education
Pendle Hill, 97
Pennsylvania, 11, 15, 19, 51, 56, 71
Pignatelli, Joe, 23, 44, 45, 49

Pilesgrove High School, 46, 47
Pilesgrove Preparative Meeting, 17
Priscilla, Bertha, 42
Progressive education, 13, 46, 81, 82
　　See also Education; Intercultural Education
Progressive Education Association, 13
Psychology, vi, 22, 29, 66, 96, 97, 99
PTA, see Parent Teacher Association
Puerto Ricans, 36, 109, 110, 112
Purgation, 100, 105

Q

Quakers, 1, 14, 45
　　conferences, 2
　　Gerald Heard, work with, 98, 99
　　history of, 97
　　infrastructure, 15
　　Rachel's Concern, 2
　　Rachel's sabbatical with, 42
　　schools, vii, 1, 17, 51
　　worship, 45

R

Race relations
　　abolitionism, 2
　　Rachel's Concern, 2, 17
　　segregation, 57
　　See also Discrimination; Ethnicity; Immigrants
Rachel, 1
　　education (early); Bucknell University (1910–1914), 2, 19, 20, 23, 51, 52, 54, 70, 101; elementary through high school (1892–1910), 19
　　education (graduate/teacher); dissertation, 32, 33, 69, 79, 89; Glassboro High School (1914–1921), 2, 20, 54–56, 133; honors, 45, 137, 138; New York University (1936–1940), 32, 69, 78, 79, 81, 87; Teacher's College, Columbia University (1929–1936), 4, 29, 78; Woodbury Assembly (see Woodbury Unified Assembly Plan); Woodbury High School (1924–1929), 4, 59, 63, 70, 77, 137–139
　　legacy; child centered education, views on, 31; overview of, 32; written work, 31–36; See also Intercultural Education
　　personal life; autobiography, 23, 32, 33, 41, 49; as chapters, 6, 7, 92; childhood, vi, 6, 18, 22, 23, 33, 41, 46, 47, 49, 53, 59, 85, 124; death, 48, 54; "Dreaming Ahead," 3, 95, 96, 106; empathy, 99; family, 1, 17, 23, 31, 41–44, 46, 51, 52, 71, 128; folklore, exposure to, vi, viii, 1, 5, 8, 12, 13, 22–28, 43, 107, 119–135; Gerald Heard Seminar, vii, 4, 36, 95; Great Segue, vii, 95–102; nature, love of, 3, 5; physically, 35, 89; as a Quaker (see under Quakers); romantically, 106, 128 (see also DuBois, Nathan Steward); socially, 51, 52, 68, 105, 121, 130; tolerance, view of, 31, 68, 73, 85, 102, 121, 127, 131
Radio programming, 26, 89
Rathje, Lisa, 28
Rauh, Joseph, 115
Religious groups
　　faction splits within, 15
　　as factor in civilization, 84
　　persecution of, 14, 15

INDEX

science, compatibility with, 96, 97, 100
  See also Judaism; Quakers
The Road to Peace, 42
Robert Simons School, 109
Roosevelt, Franklin D., 89, 107
Roosevelt, Theodore, 47
Rosenberg, Jan, 12, 128
Rosenwald, Julius, 60n7
Rugg, Harold, 13, 63, 75n1, 78
Rural schooling, 47

S

Schooling, 43
Schools
  Baptist, 19
  historically black, 58
  public, 2, 28, 32, 47, 57
  Quaker, 17
  segregation, 57
  See also Education; *individual schools*
Schwartz, Blanche, 111
Scientific method, 19, 28, 53, 70, 73
  See also Kulp, Daniel, II
Segregation
  Jim Crow, 57
  See also Integration; Race relations
Selig, Diana, 34, 68, 120
Senate Subcommittee on Government Operations, 115
Service Bureau for Intercultural Education (SBIE), vii, 2, 4, 34, 35, 69, 77–92, 106, 107, 124, 131
Sidener, Diane, 129
Situational, 67
1660 Declaration, 16
Smith, Walter Robinson, 28
Social, 66
Social construction, 3
Society of Friends, *see* Quakers

Sociology
  culture as taught (concept), 30
  education, 5, 6, 28–31, 70, 78, 85, 87, 97, 111, 132, 135
  vs. psychology, 29
Sociology of Teaching, The (Waller), 29
Spirituality, *see individual groups;* Mysticism; Religious groups
Spirituality and religion, 43
Steinberg, Milton, 93n6
Students (in Folklore and Education), 8, 25, 26
Students' families, 110
Studer, Norman, 26
Superstitions, 43

T

Taft, 47
Teachers, 110
  cooperation with folklorists, 25, 26, 28
  Parent Teacher Association (PTA), 33
  Teacher's College, Columbia University, 29
Technology, 25–26, 89
Texas, 71
Theater
  Rachel's story as, 5
  Rachel's usage of, 5
Thomas, Peg, 115
Thomas W. I., 29
Thoms, William, v, 22
Thorndike, E.L., 19, 29, 32
"Thousand—acre superfarmer," 48
Thrasher, Frederick, 87
Tolerance, 67
Tolerance, Rachel's view of, 31, 67, 68, 121, 131
Torres, Mrs., 110
Trabuco monastery, 96

Tradition bearers, 12, 25
Turkey Buzzard, 31, 43
Turkey Buzzard Dance, 43

U
Union, 100, 105

V
Value center, 127
Voorhees, SC, 17
Voorhees Normal and Industrial
    School, 57

W
Waller, Willard, 29
War, 16, 17, 55–57, 107, 108, 134
Washington, Booker T., 17
Washington, D.C., 54, 81, 115
Watson, John B., 29, 97
Weinstein, Jacob, 80
Wechsler, James, 115
Wilder, Thornton, 5
Williams, Bill, 23, 44, 45, 49
Women's International League
    For Peace and Freedom,
    58, 59, 63
Woodbury High School, 2, 63
Woodbury Unified Assembly Plan
    Rachel's dissertation about, 80
Woodstown Monthly
    Meeting, 17
Woodstown, New Jersey, 13, 17, 34,
    47, 56, 63, 119
Workshop for Cultural
    Democracy, vii, 2, 4, 36,
    105–117, 119, 124
World unity, 108

Printed in the United States
By Bookmasters